A DARK HISTORY

CHINA

A DARK HISTORY CHINA

FROM ANCIENT DYNASTIES TO THE COMMUNIST PARTY

MICHAEL KERRIGAN

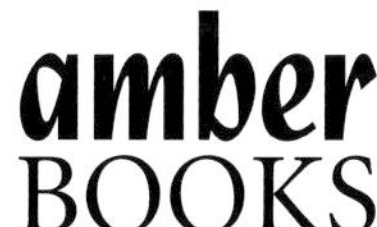

amber BOOKS

Published by
Amber Books Ltd
United House
North Road
London
N7 9DP
United Kingdom
www.amberbooks.co.uk
Instagram: amberbooksltd
Facebook: www.facebook.com/amberbooks
Pinterest: Amberbooksltd
Twitter: @amberbooks

ISBN: 978-1-78274-907-3

Project Editor: Michael Spilling
Designer: Hart-McLeod Publishing Services
Picture Research: Terry Forshaw

Printed in UAE

1 4 6 8 10 9 7 5 3 2

Contents

Introduction

The darkness in China's history has lain partly in the experiences of the country itself and partly in how these have been interpreted in the wider world.

Piled up, packed together all around, Wang Xiuchu reported, the layers of bodies stretched away 'like fish-scales' in the shadow of the city walls. The scholar went on:

The group of us were herded like sheep by a dog; anyone who lagged was whipped and beaten, or simply killed. The women were bound by their necks with a large rope, strung together like pearls on a necklace, stumbling with each step, the whole of their bodies thick with mud. Everywhere you looked, the ground was covered with infants, either crushed by horses' hooves or trampled underfoot by fleeing people. Some parents had given up their lives in sacrifice, and the sound of sobbing filled the space.

Every drainage ditch or pond we passed had layers of corpses piled up in it, their hands and feet resting on each other, and the blood flowing into the water to make it multicoloured, red and green. The canals were just level ground – so brimful were they of bodies.

Opposite: To outsiders, Chinese civilization has seemed simultaneously magnificent and mysterious. Here an 18th-century emperor (perhaps Qianlong) makes a procession.

Above: The Manchu's mythic ancestor Tada no Manchu takes on a sea-serpent in this print from the 1880s.

Wang Xiuchu's *Diary of the Ten Days of Yangzhou* describes his experiences when the city on the Yangtze, in eastern China's Jiangsu province, was attacked by Manchu forces in May 1645. His account, immediate as it is, hardly does justice to the scale of the massacre: 800,000 men, women and children may have died.

THE MURDEROUS MANCHU

Originating well to the north, in the region now known as Manchuria, the Manchu had for a long time been a subject people of China's Ming Dynasty. By the beginning of the 17th century, what had started out as a rebellion had segued into an invasion of, or encroachment into, the Chinese homeland. Having taken Liaoyang in 1621 and Shenyang four years later, the Manchu had established themselves as a new ruling dynasty for China as a whole – the Qing.

Continuing resistance as they pushed slowly southwards brought further battles and more massacres over the ensuing years. The 'Ten Days of Yangzhou' seems to have been contrived by the Qing to make an example of a city that had shown the courage to hold out against them; it represented a bloody culmination (but by no means the completion) of their conquest. Not until the 1680s would the Qing rule over the entire Chinese Empire, by which time tens of thousands more people had been killed.

DARK DAYS

A dark history of China is rich in episodes of slaughter of this sort, sometimes perpetrated by invaders like the Manchu, or by the Mongols in the 13th century. Britain's attacks in the so-called Opium Wars of the 19th century were more about humiliation than carnage, the actions of an imperialist power bullying a country into submission (and, consequently, into mercantile tractability). Even so, the episode cost several thousand Chinese lives. More directly comparable with the coming of the Manchu was the Nanjing Massacre of December 1937, when Japanese invaders killed anything up to 300,000 people, overwhelmingly civilians.

Above: The Manchu were just the latest in a succession of warlike enemies descending on the Chinese Empire from the Eurasian steppe.

China was capable of drumming up darkness of its own, too. An entire era of early Chinese history is known as the time of the Warring States on account of its chronic civil strife. The so-called Three Kingdoms period was even worse. Then there was a bitter and bloody civil war between Communists and Nationalists in the 20th century. That kind of conflict can shade imperceptibly over into state oppression, as was seen under the leadership of Chairman Mao. His Great Leap Forward (1958–62) and the famine it brought with it cost tens of millions of lives; his Cultural Revolution (1966–76) many thousands more. Since Mao's death, something like stability has returned to China. Even so, the suppression of protests by democracy campaigners in Tiananmen Square in 1989 is believed to have resulted in well over 1000 deaths.

This brings us to the violence dealt by the Chinese to others as aggressors: the occupation of Tibet, since its invasion in 1950, is the most notorious example. And although by international consensus it is a domestic issue – while an autonomous region, the Xinjiang province of western China is part of the People's Republic – its Uighur minority do not seem convinced.

China's emergence as an economic superpower in recent years has brought with it a more aggressive posture towards the outside world. Even now, the kind of open belligerence that characterized the 19th century British Empire seems alien to its character, but China has been discreetly amassing both military

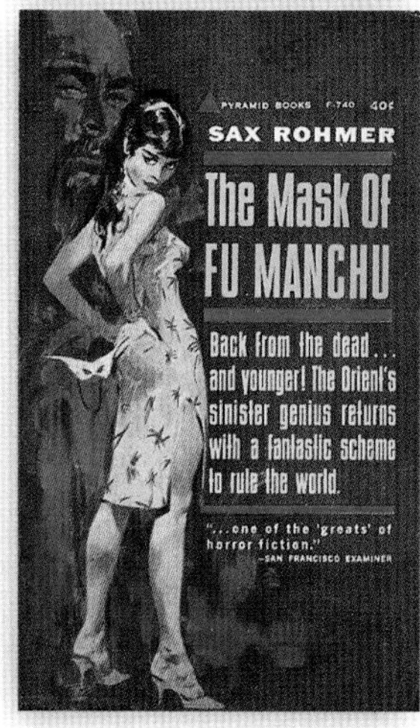

Above: Sax-Rohmer's Fu Manchu personified the stereotype of the inscrutably cunning, unfathomably evil, 'Chinaman'.

and diplomatic power. Its extensive investment program in Africa has for many observers the hallmarks of a new kind of quiet colonialism. China has also carried out espionage – industrial as well as political – and waged large-scale cyberwarfare against rival powers.

Another 'dark history' has been written largely in the West, and has been both deeply prejudiced and prejudicial. No history is free from bias, and many nations have been on the receiving end of historiographical unfairness. One example would be Spain, against which a 'Black Legend' of oppressive fanaticism was conjured up by northern Europe's Protestant powers from the 16th century. Another example can be found in accounts by Western writers of Communist Russia in the 20th century Cold War (Russian historians would return the compliment in their accounts of the 'warmongering' capitalist Western nations).

China's equivalent of the 'Black Legend' found its ultimate expression in the US 'Yellow Peril' immigrant panic of the late 19th century and in the sensationalist and racist Fu Manchu fictions of the early 20th century. Its origins can be traced back much further, though, and in one form or another the scaremongering has continued ever since.

EASTERN PROMISE, ORIENTAL THREAT

To some extent, China has experienced the same sort of prejudice that was expressed in Western thought to 'oriental' cultures of every sort, from North Africa, the Arab countries and Persia to Japan. That prejudice has been age-old. In Roman literature, it was represented in Virgil's Carthaginian Dido and her erotic hold over the hero Aeneas. Then there was the historic menace represented by the Egyptian queen Cleopatra. In both these cases, an opposition was set up between the soft seductiveness of an essentially feminine Orient – luxuriously enticing but ultimately devious and deadly – and a straightforwardly honest, dutiful and masculine Western way.

The identification of the Orient with a fatal feminine allure continued into modern times. 'Every bourgeois has considered himself capable of immense passions,' wrote the French novelist

Gustave Flaubert (1821–80). 'The most mediocre libertine has dreamed of eastern queens.' Ottoman Turkey may have been strongly patriarchal in its rule, but for Westerners it represented sexual licence. What really caught the European imagination about their all-powerful sultans was their extensive harems of wives and concubines. China, as the source of such luxuries as silk and fine porcelain, was also associated with the idea of a faintly feminized high life.

Above: A 19th century artwork of an opium den. China bore the blame for an opium threat of which it was overwhelmingly the victim.

In the aftermath of the Opium Wars, successive emperors were forced by the Royal Navy to cancel the crackdowns they had previously attempted among their people and accept unlimited British shipments of the drug. The skyrocketing rise in opium use that followed just as inevitably led to associated problems. With so big and well organized a commerce of its own, China became the world centre for the opium trade – and was naturally if unjustly demonized on that account.

Along with drug smuggling, it was assumed, went the trade in other sorts of contraband, specifically that of women for prostitution. There was indeed widespread trafficking in Chinese women, shipped to Californian brothels where they for the most part serviced their own immigrant countrymen. This was a scandal, although it does not seem to have been as upsetting to the US press as the largely imaginary 'White Slavery': it was taken for granted that evil Asiatics would lust over fair-haired Caucasian women. In so far as it existed at all, white slavery seems to have been undertaken by white slavers, but China was taken to be the centre of this trade too.

If the prejudice against China has followed the 'orientalist' pattern in obvious and important ways, in others it has gone

AN ORIENTAL UNDERWORLD

THE POPULAR WRITER ARTHUR Conan Doyle (1859–1930) understood the Anglo-Saxon sensibilities of his time. The scene-setting for his Sherlock Holmes story, 'The Man with the Twisted Lip' (1891), is interesting in the way it seems to sum up contemporary English anxieties about China.

Holmes' assistant, Doctor Watson, is asked by a concerned woman to find her missing husband who has, she fears, lost himself in a self-destructive stupor in an opium den. The Bar of Gold, as this notorious dive is called, lies down by the docks 'in the farthest east of the City' (in a sort of London orient, it could be said). Watson's mission takes him to a 'vile alley, lurking behind...high wharves'. The place he is looking for lies, we're told, 'between a slop-shop and a gin-shop'. Given that a 'slop-shop' was what we'd now call a sweatshop, while a 'gin-shop' catered to the most despised sort of homegrown alcohol addiction, this street was already a sort of Victorian English urban hell.

But Watson's quest takes him still lower, down 'a steep flight of steps leading...to a black gap like the mouth of a cave'. A few years later, Sigmund Freud (1856–1939) would have done the groundwork for Conan Doyle's readers to be able to see this awful aperture as a symbolic *vagina dentata* – literally, the 'toothed vagina' that bites off and emasculates the phallus it entices in. Even without psychoanalytical assistance, educated Victorians would have recognized this as a version of the classical *katabasis* – the 'going down' of the ancient epics, in which heroes such as Odysseus (the *Odyssey*, XI) or Aeneas (the *Aeneid*, VI) descend into the realms of the dead in search of enlightenment.

HELLISH INFERNO

What Dr Watson finds in this oriental underworld, however, bears more resemblance to the infernal vision of a medieval poet such as Dante (c. 1265–1321) or a painter like Hieronymus Bosch (1450–1516):

Through the gloom one could dimly catch a glimpse of bodies lying in strange fantastic poses, bowed shoulders, bent knees, heads thrown back, and chins pointing upward, with here and there a dark, lack-lustre eye turned upon the newcomer. Out of the black shadows there glimmered little red circles of light, now bright, now faint, as the burning poison waxed or waned in the bowls of the metal pipes. The most lay silent, but some muttered to themselves, and others talked together in a strange, low, monotonous voice, their conversation coming in gushes, and then suddenly tailing off into silence, each mumbling out his own thoughts and paying little heed to the words of his neighbour.

Above: A slave-girl dressed in holiday attire, San Francisco, c. 1900.

significantly further. Chinese life, society and culture have been perceived as being at some deep level inhuman, and not just by sensationalist novelists and journalists but by serious and knowledgeable commentators from the West. It was not considered less than human (so many centuries of Chinese civilization was impossible to ignore), but anti-human, which was in some ways worse.

Take this passage from *A Journey Through the Chinese Empire* (1854) in which the writer, the French Catholic missionary Évariste Régis Huc (1813–60), describes a trial:

The first object that presented itself on entering this Chinese judgment hall was the accused...

He was suspended in the middle of the hall, like one of those lanterns, of whimsical form and colossal dimensions often seen in the great pagodas. Ropes attached to a great beam in the roof held him tied by the wrists and feet, so as to throw the body into the form of a bow. Beneath him stood five or six executioners, armed with rattan rods and leather lashes, in ferocious attitudes, their clothes and faces spotted with blood – the blood of the unfortunate creature, who was uttering stifled groans, while his flesh was torn almost in tatters. The audience present at this frightful spectacle appeared quite at their ease.... Many laughed, indeed, at the horror visible in our faces.

This description presents as eyewitness testimony, its first-hand immediacy the guarantee of its authenticity – and we have no good grounds to dismiss it as untrue. However, the way that Huc delivers his account – its terms, its emphases, the way it is presented for his reader – might make us wonder about its intent.

In the first place, the impersonality of the defendant's description, as an 'object', reflects the inhumanity of the Chinese institution (although it is the European writer who employs the word). The architectural comparisons (lanterns, pagodas) remind

Above: Chinese civilization seemed out of step with a modernizing world. These officials ran foreign policy during the First Sino-Japanese War in 1894.

us of the sophisticated technological achievements of this society, and the fact that we're not among 'savages' arguably makes the cruelty seem worse. The way the suffering body, strung up on its cat's cradle of ropes, seems to be incorporated into the very structure of the building suggests that oppression and torture are constructional elements in Chinese culture and the Chinese state. The spots of blood on the executioners' clothes and faces reflect the moral stain on a society whose members can look on, 'quite at their ease', while a fellow human is flayed alive. The sympathy displayed by the visitors is met with scornful derision. The implication is clear: the Chinese are devoid of all compassion.

THE 'INSCRUTABILITY' ISSUE

The suggestion of China's inhumanity had been made before, by a Catholic missionary, the Italian Jesuit priest Martino Martini (1614–61). The Jesuits in general had got on well with the Chinese, who had welcomed them for their immense learning in science and technology as well as in the arts, and for the respect they had shown for Chinese achievements in these fields. Martini was no exception, and his relations with his hosts were evidently warm. Even so, he was struck by the openness of manner he saw in the Manchu. They 'rejoice to see strangers,' he noted. 'They in no way like the grimness and sourness of the Chinese gravity, and therefore they appear more human in their manner.'

Above: Martino Martini got on well with both the Chinese and their Manchu conquerors.

The Manchu were certainly not more 'human' in their behaviour, as Martini must have known. His comments appear in his *Bellum Tartaricum, Or the Conquest of the Great and Most Renowned Empire of China by the Invasion of the Tartars* (1654), his history of this particularly bloody and cruel invasion.

This suggests that Martini was talking about questions of immediate personal presentation. Somehow, it seems, the Chinese came across as not quite 'human' to Europeans who met them – even to Europeans as well disposed as Martini was. One reason for this might be some basic physical differences, which might make Chinese people's facial expressions hard for Westerners to read. The most striking of these would be the epicanthic fold to the upper lid that distinguishes the eyes of East Asians from those of Africans and Europeans. But the Manchu were of East Asian origin themselves.

The Singaporean writer, statesman and diplomat Lee Khoon Choy (1924–2016) has addressed the inscrutability question head-on. He acknowledges the existence of the 'problem' from the Western perspective but suggests that it has a cultural origin. 'For centuries,' he says,

a Chinese gentleman has not been supposed to disclose his inner feelings and emotions in his facial expression nor ever to show either happiness or anger on his face. He must have complete control over his feelings and must never allow his opponent to know what he is thinking and feeling.

Above: Martini's 1655 map of Peking (modern-day Beijing) demonstrates the deepening western understanding of the Chinese scene that he himself had worked hard to promote.

This anti-histrionic fastidiousness might explain the nervous laughter of those who witnessed the horror 'visible in the faces' of Évariste Régis Huc and his companions. It is not so different, perhaps, from the 'stoicism' embraced by the patrician class of ancient Rome. In classical society too, the duties, skills and institutions of public life were held in great importance, along with the need to conceal private feeling. The Roman might feel any number of deep emotions inwardly but these were never to be displayed in public in the Forum or the Senate.

Since ancient times, public service in China had been not just important but socially defining. Mandarin was originally the language of officialdom. Later Western accounts were to caricature the country as a vast, all-powerful bureaucracy with a nation of people only incidentally attached. And it was true to the extent that the civil service exam, introduced during the Han Dynasty in the third century CE, had become the primary determinant of social rank.

CONFUCIAN CONFUSION

Lee Khoon Choy tentatively suggests that Chinese 'inscrutability' may stem from the teachings of Confucius. It is universally agreed that K'ung Fu-Tzu, or Confucius (551–479 BCE), was the founding father of Chinese philosophical and social thinking, but precisely what he stood for is more difficult to say. The veneration he has received through more than two millennia has appeared all but religious, but he was more a moral teacher than a god. If he could be said to have founded a religion, it is the tradition of Taoism (or Daoism; 'the Way') – the belief that an overarching natural order underpins every sphere of existence, from the cosmic to the ethical. Even as a secular sage, Confucius is not easy to pin down. Rulers must lead by example, the great teacher said, in kindness, uprightness, decorum, wisdom and faithfulness. In return, their subjects had a duty to respect their authority and to serve society as a whole.

Below: A sculpture of Confucius in the Temple of Confucius in Beijing. Confucius has embodied the spirit of Chinese wisdom for 2500 years.

Confucius shared with Aristotle (384–322 BCE) an enthusiasm for the mean; the central 'pivot' upon which a proper equilibrium could be established in every aspect of existence. For Confucius, as for the Greek philosopher, excess and insufficiency end up much the same: 'The ideal virtue,' he said, 'conforms strictly to the mean.'

This doctrine did not necessarily mean an acceptance of mediocrity, but it undoubtedly encouraged a more cautious and conservative approach to life. Confucius showed a strong preference for the tried and tested approach ('when we have to carve an axe handle, the pattern we need to use is not far off') and a converse resistance to the over-adventurous or extravagant. 'The path is not far from man,' he said. 'Whenever someone tries to follow a path which takes them any distance from that of everyday common sense, this cannot possibly be seen as the right path.'

A willingness to strike out from the paths appointed by the 'everyday common sense' consensus is almost the definition of the sort of independent-mindedness and originality that have

AN INVECTIVE OF ENVY

THE ENGLISH WRITER THOMAS de Quincey (*see right*, 1785–1859) is celebrated as the author of *Confessions of an English Opium-Eater* (1821). In other writings, however, he waged a one-man war against the Chinese, despite knowing very little of the country and its culture. Throughout the period of the Opium Wars, de Quincey kept up a polemical commentary as striking in its emotional intensity as in its wrong-headedness.

In the literary scholar Diane Simmons' interpretation of these writings, the Chinese come to be a stand-in for the absent father (he was a much-travelled merchant) and cold mother who had let de Quincey down. 'In his fabrication of an Asian persona,' Simmons says, 'in his manic attacks upon a people about whom he knows virtually nothing, we see an author obsessively, if unconsciously, reliving the fury of a child at the cold, withholding omnipotence of the parent.'

De Quincey's fury makes him an outlier, perhaps, but his sense of China's quasi-parental strength and seniority is still significant, and representative of its time. While English imperialists at the time of the Opium Wars seem to have revelled in their ability to bully an essentially defenceless foreign nation, they also seem to have felt some inadequacy in the face of China's sheer size and its long history.

China's civilization, de Quincey complains, is so venerable that it can't be taken away from it; the country is so big that it is inherently invulnerable. Britain, by contrast, was an up-and-coming and as yet unproven empire based on a small and unprotected island. What went for the school playground went for imperial geopolitics, it seems: the bully at some level saw himself as a victim.

been so highly prized in Western thought. This tradition sees the individual as only being truly authentic in the extent to which he or she is autonomous and independent of society, its pressures and its norms.

The political scientist C.B. Macpherson (1911–87) in the 1960s articulated this sort of selfhood and memorably described it as 'possessive individualism', but its classic proclamation had come much earlier. In his poem 'Invictus' (1888), William Ernest Henley (1849–1903) had asserted: 'I am the master of my fate,/I am the captain of my soul.'

'THE EXECUTIONER PUTS HIS HAND INTO A COVERED BASKET IN WHICH ARE A NUMBER OF KNIVES...'

That no one can *really* claim to be either of those things is neither here nor there: this posture of existential self-sufficiency is one to which Westerners have at least learned to aspire. In the process, they have rejected an alternative understanding of individuality, which is arguably at least as valid. In the Confucian tradition, a person's integrity, authenticity and sense of self are only underlined by the appreciation that they are thinking and acting in harmony with society and the wider culture. To be true to one's community is in important ways to be true to oneself. Conversely, to privilege one's own personal interests, or even one's emotions over those of others, involves a sort of self-estrangement in the longer term.

A THOUSAND CUTS

Huc's missionary successors vied with one another in their efforts to evoke the cruelty of a Chinese justice system that seemed to them representative of the inhumanity of the culture as a whole. Hence the account by William Lockhart (1811–96), author of the autobiographical *The Medical Missionary in China* (1861), of what was officially called the 'slow and painful death'. It was, he wrote, 'inflicted in this manner':

The executioner puts his hand into a covered basket in which are a number of knives, marked with the names of various limbs and parts of the body, and drawing out one at random, he cuts off the part indicated from the body of the victim.

This is just one of many lurid descriptions of what became known as the 'death by a thousand cuts'. Other versions make it sound more sadistic, emphasizing the innumerable tiny incisions made by the executioner as he sliced away thin sections of living flesh. Lockhart's manner is brisk by contrast, his delivery deadpan, but if his tone is less sensationalist it is every bit as damning.

Like Huc before him, Lockhart sees the prisoner's plight as somehow exemplifying the structure of the society that has condemned him – in this case, the impersonality of its bureaucratic systems. Although what was officially known as *lingchi* was practised from around the 10th century to the turn of the 20th, when the empire finally fell, it happened much more often in myth and anecdote (including in Chinese myth and anecdote) than in actual fact. Today in the West the phrase 'death by a thousand cuts' is used as a metaphor. That was probably true in China too: state punishments have their symbolic functions as well as their practicalities. This kind of execution acted out the slow deliberation and complete power of the justice system.

Below: Execution 'by a thousand cuts', though by no means entirely mythical, has loomed disproportionately large in the imagination of the West.

If it acted out its heartlessness too in a way that seemed horrifying to foreign visitors, their shock was to some extent misplaced. The Western justice systems of the time could also seem cruel – especially in the Anglo-Saxon world. The legal scholar Jedidiah Joseph Kroncke has pointed out that many 19th-century criticisms of the Chinese system (not just its cruelty but its corruption and openness to bribery) reflect those being made of homegrown Anglo-American systems. Britain, for example, had only recently begun reforming the infamous 'Bloody Code' that had set the death penalty for scores of often comparatively minor offences. There was a new emphasis on the idea of the rule of law. The legal system, reformers had come to think, should set a standard of fairness for society as a whole, not just be a way of handing down punishments upon the poor.

Above: The Chinese cangue had to be carried about like a portable pillory. This prisoner couldn't even feed himself.

'THE MAD OFFICIAL'

In Western perceptions, Chinese society became a byword for bureaucracy – and, increasingly, for a civil service that existed solely to serve itself. Its pronouncements were divorced from action; its documents full of empty formulas, like the 'set phrases' one missionary complained of in 1833:

Chinese official documents abound with set phrases, which by their constant recurrence become exceedingly wearisome.... The word 'order', or 'command' will frequently occur ten or twenty times in a document of as many lines.

However, it is clear that many Western attacks upon the Chinese way articulated unease with what was happening at home. In the industrializing West, the extension of bureaucracy had been the inevitable (and, in many ways, desirable) accompaniment to economic and social development and growth, but it had brought with it new inconveniences and incongruities.

The writer G.K. Chesterton (1874–1936) made the comparison explicit when, in 1912, he attacked the imprisonment of a labourer's wife from Lambourne, Essex. Poor and sick herself, she and her husband had been living in a cottage without water supply. She was, however, sent down for the 'neglect' of their five children (all, an inspector reported, 'exceedingly well in health'), who were left motherless without her for six weeks while she served her term. 'I know no name for this but Chinese,' Chesterton writes.

It calls up the mental picture of some archaic and changeless Eastern Court, in which men with dried faces and stiff ceremonial costumes perform some atrocious cruelty to the accompaniment of formal proverbs and sentences of which the

UNCHANGING TIMES

WESTERN CONDESCENSION FACED A challenge when it came to a Chinese Empire that WAS DEMONSTRABLY HEIR TO many centuries of civilization and cultural and technological achievement. One classic way around this was to acknowledge those accomplishments but damn the Chinese for having allowed themselves to become, in the words of one early missionary, William Milne (1785–1822), the 'blind slaves of antiquity'. Milne magnanimously admitted that there had been many excellences in their ancient system:

The huge machine of their government has been often battered, both from without and from within, and still its essential parts hang together.

But, he went on,

For ages, the arts and sciences in China have been stationary; and from the accounts of the last English embassy, seem, at present, rather in a retrograde state. The obstinate refusal of the Chinese to improve, is rather to be viewed as the effect of principle, than the want of genius. They consider the ancient sages, kings, and governments, as the prototypes of excellence; and a near approximation to the times in which they lived, the highest display of national wisdom and virtue. They are still the blind slaves of antiquity, and possess not that greatness of character which sees its own defects, and sighs after improvement.

As the 19th century wore on and the Industrial Revolution strengthened its hold on the Western economies, the imperative to change in the name of progress became more pronounced. Darwin's theory of evolution – its doctrine of 'the survival of the fittest' spun to support an assumption that might was right and wealth a proof of worth – was taken as a scientific proof of the need for social change.

very meaning has been forgotten. ...But I fear I interrupt.... The boiling oil is boiling; and the Tenth Mandarin is already reciting the 'Seventeen Serious Principles and the Fifty-three Virtues of the Sacred Emperor'.

China – or at least a stereotypically imagined 'China' – had become a stick with which to beat Western countries for Western wrongs.

However, there was another China: one that was not mainly a metaphor; one that had its own existence, independent of the Western mind. It is that geographically and historically existing entity that is the subject of this book. The trouble is that the other, imagined one, keeps getting in the way. The obvious answer – to ignore it – does not make sense in historiographical practice. Western perceptions were to have an enormous, and often damaging, impact on the real country over the centuries. Any study of Chinese history has to take account of both these countries.

Below: Prisoners prostrate themselves before a judge and his officials, 1885. Chinese courts were reputedly both harsh and corrupt.

1

CHINA BEFORE CHINA

China's prehistory is 'dark' chiefly in the sense that it is almost completely obscure, while its early written history is strongly tinged with myth.

TOOLS EXCAVATED at Shangchen on the Loess (or Huangtu) Plateau around the Wei River Valley in west-central China's Shaanxi and Shanxi provinces appear to date back more than two million years. This puts the hominids who made them well before the emergence of present-day *Homo sapiens* out of Africa. Even so-called 'Peking Man', of whom fossil remains were found at the Zhoukoudian Caves outside Beijing, is believed to have represented another earlier type. *Homo erectus* flourished some 750,000 years ago before disappearing from the Earth, supplanted, or simply replaced, perhaps many millennia later, by *Homo sapiens*.

The earliest actual humans, in the Paleolithic era, lived in small communities of nomadic hunter-gatherers. That meant travelling light, living from day to day, and leaving only the scantiest traces behind them. It has been almost impossible for archaeologists to identify these. Only with the advent of agriculture and the formation of sedentary communities in the

Opposite: Attendants wait while a woman entertains the Zhou King Mu on a zither-like *guzheng*. China already had a splendid civilization in the 10th century BCE.

Neolithic era do we find any significant record being left. Modern researchers have found evidence of rice being grown at Bashidang, in the Yangtze Valley, from around 8000 BCE, and of millet cultivation at Cishan, in the Yellow River Valley, from around 6000 BCE.

It is only with the formation of such settlements, and the opportunity they bring to accumulate surpluses – and accordingly the amassing of wealth and prestige – that history really has the chance to become 'dark'. We think of farming as peaceful work, but the channelling of a designated peasantry's productivity into agriculture allows the freeing up of a minority to become aristocratic warriors, soldiers, scribes or officials and craftworkers who create the luxury possessions that become the signs of wealth. This wealth, being portable – as grain, livestock or luxuries – can consequently be hoarded, or stolen in acts of war. Local magnates create rudimentary states around themselves.

Above: This cross-patterned shield was made during the Xia Dynasty (c. 2070–1600 BCE).

THE XIA: FROM SELF-SACRIFICE TO TYRANNY

The first of these early states in China appears to have been ruled by the Xia Dynasty, which traditionally reigned in the neighbourhood of what is now Zhengzhou, in central China's Henan province. Its rulers were supposedly in power from around 2070 to 1600 BCE, and its history was overshadowed by a 'Great Flood', for which some archaeological evidence exists. Yu, the founder of the Xia, is held to have worked for thirteen years digging a channel to divert the Yellow River, finally averting the threat it posed to the people of his kingdom. Throughout that time he never managed to return to his palace once. The Xia's last king, Jie, was every bit as villainous as

Opposite: As founder of the Xia Dynasty, Yu's authority rested on his having saved his realms from flooding – a key responsibility of Chinese rulers throughout history.

Yu had been saintly; the two were to be held up as contrasting types in Chinese chronicles ever after. So closely did they conform to these appointed roles that it is difficult to avoid the suspicion that they may have been entirely mythical figures.

Historical or not, Jie certainly became a focus for negative mythology. The ultimate tyrant, he is said to have made his ministers and courtiers crouch down so he could ride around on them like horses. He had an appropriately wicked helpmeet in his concubine, Mo Xi – lovely in looks, it is said, but utterly depraved. Despite her feminine beauty, she had no respect for the gendered proprieties that went with it: she wore a sword at her waist and the cap of a warrior on her head. She also had an unladylike love of alcohol, which matched her husband's. The story goes that she begged him to create a whole lake of wine, which they then sailed around on in a boat. Having tired of this game, they had 3000 of King Jie's courtiers get down on their hands and knees in the shallows to drink the lake dry. As each became intoxicated, he toppled in and drowned, much to the amusement of the royal couple.

THE ADVENT OF THE SHANG

Jie's reign is supposed to have brought the Xia era to an end – in some versions of the mythic story, he was betrayed by Mo Xi. She was said to have been

Right: Human sacrifice was central to the religious life of the Shang era: these skulls were excavated in the modern city of Zhengzhou.

Opposite: Mei Bo, King Zhou's prime minister (above) and the royal consort, the cruel Daji, below, from a relief at Ping Sien Si temple, Malaysia.

having an affair with one Yi Yin, chief counsellor to King Tang (c. 1675–1600 BCE). Tang appears to have been the founder of the Shang Dynasty – one for which there is rather more archaeological support.

Unfortunately, excavations do not bear out the legend that Tang was as self-sacrificing as his predecessor Yu had been: the story goes that he offered to have himself killed to appease the angry gods who had hit his kingdom with a fearsome drought. However, archaeologists have found that the priests of the Shang pursued a policy of human sacrifice. Victims were variously beheaded, dismembered, cut in half, bled, beaten or chopped to death. Inscriptions found by researchers commemorate at least 14,000 such rituals – the vast majority of those slaughtered appear to have been young males.

The remains of more than a thousand sacrificial victims have been found thrown together in pits in a single cemetery outside the old Shang capital, Yin (or Yinxu), near Anyang; others seem to have been placed in tombs and the foundations of new buildings as offerings. Fu Hao (c. 1200 BCE), a queen and high priestess, was laid to rest in a rich and splendid tomb in Yinxu, alongside an extremely impressive treasure hoard. Together with hundreds of bronze and ceramic vessels, precious jewellery of jade and ivory and thousands of cowrie shells (which were used as currency), she had with her fifteen human skeletons.

A CRUEL KING

Tang's legendary status as a saintly ruler is important because it underlines the parallels between the stories of his dynasty and Yu's Xia. Mythohistory repeated itself towards the mid-11th century BCE when a Jie-like tyrant, Di Xin or Zhou, came to the throne. Although blessed with every gift, and indeed a benevolent enough ruler to start with, he later lapsed into drunken womanizing and cruelty. At his open-air orgies, he forced naked young boys and girls to perform obscene dances under trees whose branches had been hung with joints of meat. He was a glutton for flesh of every kind, it seems.

Zhou too was urged on in his descent into viciousness by a favourite concubine, the dreaded Daji. Some sources represent her as a cunning, evil, fox-spirit. Like Mo Xi before her, Daji seems to have had a sadistic sense of fun.

THE 'BURNING PILLAR'

IT WAS APPARENTLY AT Daji's request that King Zhou had his infamous *Paolao* or burning pillar designed. This giant bronze cylinder was set up above a layer of flattened charcoal. The cylinder's curving surface was coated with viscous oil, and the unfortunate victim was made to stand on it barefoot while the charcoal was set on fire. As the flames beneath it rose, the bronze grew progressively hotter and its slimy surface ever more difficult to stand on. Shifting his feet in hopes of gaining relief, the prisoner found himself struggling and slithering ever more frantically – until at last he fell into the blazing bed below. Daji, the sources tell us, was sexually aroused at the sight of suffering like this; her king was brought to ecstasy by the sight of her arousal.

Above: King Wu was the founder of the Zhou Dynasty (1046–225 BCE).

She encouraged Zhou in his experiments, which included the dismemberment and pickling in brine of counsellors who had criticized him. Mei Bo, the king's prime minister, had been the nearest thing the Shang state had to a steadying hand under Zhou's chaotic rule. Inevitably, Daji saw him as a threat. She pestered the king until he at last sent Mei Bo to suffer the torture of the 'burning pillar', and from that time on the kingdom fell apart.

THE ZHOU DYNASTY

Heaven, the scholars subsequently insisted, brought about the downfall of King Zhou and the Shang Dynasty. Its immediate instrument, however, was the son of his former counsellor, Ji Chang. He had arguably fared well in emerging from his royal service with his life. Even so, he had been arbitrarily imprisoned by King Zhou. Now his vengeful son Wu raised an army and marched against the Shang. Wu's forces were victorious at the Battle of Muye (c. 1046 BCE). The humiliated king returned to his palace, draped himself in all his regal finery and jewellery and set himself on fire. His vanquisher seized the throne and reigned as King Wu. Although no relation of the tyrant-king (their names are not the same in Chinese script or speech), he called the new dynasty he had established the Zhou.

This came to be called the 'Western Zhou', as it ruled from Wu's new capital, Fenghao, in Shaanxi province, where the River Feng flows into the Wei River. The Zhou were ultimately to rule for seven centuries, although after the first few generations their authority seemed pretty much spent, as feudal vassals across their empire began to bully them. The beauty of the Zhou system had been its looseness, its rulers devolving a great deal of power to nobles in the different regions of their realm. They took the resources of the country, and the productive labours of its people, and gave their loyalty to the Zhou ruler in return.

This worked well for a time, as long as royal sovereignty at the centre could be backed militarily when needed. But the nobles, wealthy as they were, became accustomed to being little kings at local level, and increasingly wayward in their relationship with the monarchy. By the beginning of the eighth century, the nobles were actively scheming to seize power themselves, and in 771 they made common cause with the Quan Rong, nomadic raiders from the Steppes to the north. Rising up in revolt against their Zhou rulers, they succeeded in capturing Fenghao, bringing to an end the era of the Western Zhou. The royal household fled to safety, establishing a new capital further east at Luoyang. But although the Eastern Zhou Dynasty was to last 500 years (from 770 to 256 BCE),

Below: An eagle on his wrist, a modern-day steppe nomad hunts on horseback.

'DOG BARBARIANS'

To the Chinese, the Quan Rong were 'Dog Barbarians' – in part for the obvious, pejorative reasons, although the Quan Rong seem to have revered the dog as a totem animal and had a dog's head as their sign. The nomadic herders of the northern steppe were to be an issue for Chinese civilization for centuries – at best an irritant; at worst (with attacks by the Mongols and the Manchu) an all but existential threat.

All the settled communities in the regions round the edges of the Eurasian steppe despised the nomads. What passed for their economic model – moving their flocks around from place to place as water supplies and grazing fluctuated – never gave them much more than the most meagre level of subsistence. On the other hand, the fact that this poverty caused them constantly to look elsewhere for making up deficits and securing extra luxuries was always ominous.

The nomads' lifestyle on the steppe had, moreover, fostered immense toughness and supreme horsemanship skills. They had an extraordinary facility with the short bows they could shoot at a gallop, while wheeling and turning at a moment's notice. The histories of the great civilizations not just of the Far East but also of India, Persia, the Middle East, the Mediterranean and Western Europe were all to be punctuated by the invasions of steppe nomads of one sort or another.

it continued to be beset by the same problems. Its rulers were in practice little more than figureheads: real power was held – and fiercely fought over – by the leading nobles.

Below: In the Period of the Warring States, even money took the form of weaponry: knives like these were used as currency.

THE 'MIDDLE KINGDOM'

By 700 BCE, the Eastern Zhou empire comprised well over a hundred separate statelets, each with its own urban centre from which a local king or warlord wielded power. Many of these kingdoms were tiny (even at their most extensive, Zhou dominions never covered anything like all of what we now think of as China), yet their rulers prized their independence just the same. Collectively, these kingdoms referred to themselves as the *Zhongguo* – literally, 'the states of the Middle', a name said to stem from their inhabitants' comfortable assumption that their homeland lay at the centre of the earth.

To the north, they knew, was an endless arid expanse across which nomadic herding peoples roamed – and from which all too often they struck southward, invading and pillaging border regions. To the south lay tropical forests whose tribes seemed utterly alien to the Chinese, although they valued many of the products the jungles yielded.

Slowly but surely, a recognizably Chinese culture began to emerge in the Middle Kingdom – yet political coherence still seemed a distant dream. In what became known as the 'Spring and Autumn' period (from the name of a chronicle that claimed to report its various ups and downs) quarrels erupted and alliances shifted with bewildering speed. 'Everything is ravaged and destroyed,' one king complained. 'All are full of sorrow and sadness and do not know how to protect themselves.'

Even now, moreover, no equilibrium had been reached. A sort of stability was attained as the anarchy of the fifth century shook down to the extent that seven larger states started to emerge from the confusion. Han, Wei, Zhao, Qi, Yan, Chu and Qin all dwarfed the much-diminished kingdom of Zhou – whose rulers, however, remained their nominal overlords. But the situation was anything but peaceful. Indeed, the conflict between these leading kingdoms (along with smaller coastal states such as Lu and Wu) only intensified in what Chinese history calls the Period of the Warring States (453–221 BCE).

CENTRALIZING STATES

The rulers of this period knew too well the dangers of an over-powerful nobility – they themselves had risen at the expense of their overlords. Therefore, they shunned the arm's-length approach of the Zhou in favour of a direct despotism, concentrating power and prestige around their own persons and their courts. To cut out the aristocratic interest further, they drew their counsellors from the lower ranks of the aristocracy – the beginnings, it might be said, of a civil service. Academies were established to train up this cohort of bureaucrats, instilling in them the virtues of orderliness and obedience. The foundations for Confucianism were being prepared. The sage himself was to grow up in the little state of Lu, in the Shandong province of today. It was ruled by cousins of the kings of Zhou.

Above: The young Confucius guides his playmates to the rightful path.

Scientific study was fostered: any technological advance might bestow an edge in economic prowess, or an advantage on the battlefield. The demotion of the old elite extended into the military realm. Once war had been the business of a few great warriors, heroic figures in their mighty chariots, their clashes a chivalrous, almost ritualized affair. Now this knightly class was sidelined, the work of warfare falling instead to vast armies of

low-born and expendable infantry. They were forced to fight to the death, in what was more like modern 'total war', under the direction of a new breed of ruthless and resourceful generals.

FROM BRONZE TO IRON

It is no surprise that a period of ceaseless conflict should have been a time of rapid innovation in the military sphere. As armies fought back and forth across each other's territories, they acquired new skills in siege warfare and fortification; the advent of the crossbow transformed the battlefield. Even allowing for exaggeration on the chroniclers' part, reports of armies many tens of thousand strong abound, suggesting an impressive degree of organization, not only in the field but also in logistical support. The equipping of such armies would have required production on a massive scale.

The advent of ironworking helped. For some time, Chinese smiths had been making bronze with high iron content for extra durability; now iron became the catalyst of an industrial revolution. The addition of carbon in the form of charcoal allowed iron to be cast from molten ore, using high-temperature ovens originally developed for the manufacture of specialized bronze and ceramic products. Cast-iron items could readily be mass-produced, though the metal was too brittle to make effective tools or weaponry. Traditional forging methods were still used in the preparation of these, but efficient administration allowed smiths to be mobilized in their thousands.

The skill and labour required to build the impressive fortifications that were a feature of this period were also as much a triumph of centralized organization as of engineering. These were not just city walls or fortresses: giant walls of compacted mud, sun-dried brick and sometimes stone snaked for miles across vulnerable border areas. At a time when each state lived in suspicion of its neighbours – and all dreaded the onslaught of nomadic raiders – the need for such fortified frontiers was clear.

Left: The beauty of this bronze sword reminds us that, in ancient China as in other times, warfare was a proud – and often glamorous – way of life.

On the one hand, Chinese civilization, technology and governance were coming on in leaps and bounds; on the other, all its creative energies were going into waging war.

THE CONQUERING QIN

Slowly, painfully, bloodily, as decades of attrition turned to centuries, the general conflict was inching its way towards resolution. Out of all these sparring, squabbling states, a single winner was emerging, ready to take all in the war for pre-eminence in the Middle Kingdom. By tradition founded in 897 BCE, Qin had risen in the northwest in what is now Gansu province. In 314 BCE, a memorable victory over the Quan Rong nomads had brought a vast expanse of new territory within its borders. Two years later, it had scored important victories over

THE ART OF WAR

'VICTORS WIN FIRST, THEN go to war; losers go to war then try to win.' A typical rhetorical rapier thrust from the inimitable Sun Tzu (or Sunzi, 544–496 BCE), whose *The Art of War* has influenced military strategy ever since. Sun Tzu's special wisdom seems applicable in other fields too, from sport to modern management theory.

Sun Tzu was above all an advocate of subtlety: 'The summit of skill is to win without fighting,' he insisted. 'Always leave a surrounded enemy an escape-route,' he warned. 'Treat your soldiers as you would your sons,' he said. 'Do not demand victory from your men,' he counselled: 'Create a situation in which your triumph is inevitable.'

THE ART OF WAR ILLUSTRATED
SUN TZU

Not much is known of the man himself; it is not even certain whether he actually existed or was just a composite of several different, and anonymous, scribes. The later historian Sima Qian (c. 145–85 BCE) suggested that Sun Tzu had been a real general in the service of the King of Wu, whose (vastly outnumbered) forces he had led to victory over those of Chu at the Battle of Bofu (506 BCE), before the period of the Warring States was under way. Contemporary chroniclers do not confirm this claim, however. Modern scholars generally agree that, whoever their author may have been, these writings probably date from the fifth century BCE.

the Ba and Shu kingdoms in what we know as Sichuan, and secured further conquests from the Han kingdom to the east.

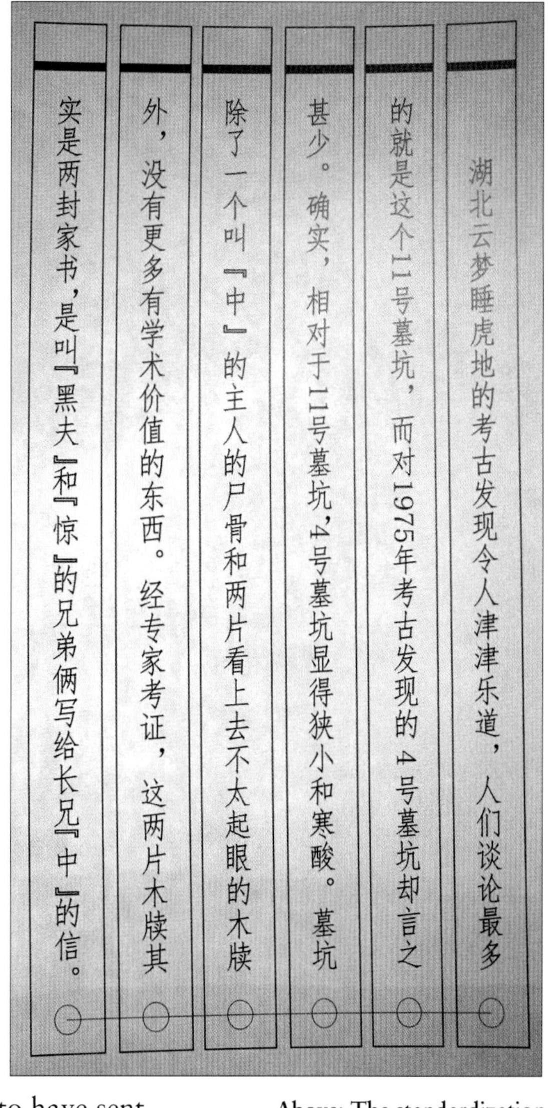

Above: The standardization of script was one of many regularizing measures that helped enable the Qin Dynasty to govern China as a single state.

Opposite: Sun Tzu embodies important qualities of self-confidence, subtlety and cunning.

Its situation in this frontier region had arguably given it space to expand and room to manoeuvre: whatever the reason, it was in the ascendant by the third century. Qin is transliterated into English script as 'Ch'in' – the initial 'q' represents a 'ch' sound – and it is from this word that the modern name of China is derived. The country was to become the basis for the modern Chinese state.

Before that, however, the mounting menace it posed stretched the other states to their breaking points. The kingdom of Zhao, for example, had conscripted all males of fifteen and over into its army. Who was going to work the fields? War throughout the ancient world was a seasonal occupation, but even so the costs of all this conflict for beleaguered states could not be long sustained. As many as a million men may have been in the field when Zhao and Qin forces met at Changping, not far from Gaoping, in Shanxi province, in 260 BCE.

Before the battle, the Qin leadership is said to have sent secret agents into Zhao to spread rumours that their general, Lian Po, was contemplating retreat, afraid that he might lose his life in the coming fight. We cannot know how effective this early example of what we'd now call 'psy ops' was, but Bai Qi's Qin forces prevailed.

Bai Qi was at once a gloriously successful and a notoriously cruel commander. It was on his orders, it is said, that, after the battle (in the course of which no fewer than 50,000 soldiers had fallen on the Zhao side), a further 400,000 prisoners were buried alive.

2

Imperial Power

The 'First Divine Emperor', Shihuangdi, rolled China's jostling, squabbling little kingdoms up into a single state, its territories stretching from Central Asia to Vietnam.

The defeat of Zhao left the kingdom of Qin with no serious rival in the Middle Kingdom, but this pre-eminence was not the same as imperial sway. It took Ying Zheng (258–210 BCE) to enforce his authority on Qin, and Qin's on the country as a whole. He is remembered as Shihuangdi, 'First Divine Emperor', the title he bestowed upon himself in 221 BCE.

Ying Zheng's reign did not get off to the most promising start, and neither had his father's. Although King Zhuang Xiang (281–247 BCE) had ultimately been an adequate ruler, his path to the throne had been dubious. The illegitimate son of a royal prince, he had seemed marked out for marginalization and then oblivion.

Zhuang Xiang had been sent away from Xianyang, Qin's capital, to live in a neighbouring state as a semi-permanent hostage – a guarantee against attack (a common diplomatic device in these still troubled times). There he became a protégé

Opposite: Standing at the ready for two millennia and more, the troops of the 'Terracotta Army' bear impressive testimony to imperial China's wealth and strength.

of the king's first minister, Lü Buwei (291–235 BCE). This ambitious and unscrupulous former merchant saw in the young man the opportunity to rise still further and busied himself getting the young man into his debt. He even 'gave' the prince his favourite concubine, Lady Zhao (c. 280–228 BCE).

REGENCY CRISIS

Lady Zhao subsequently bore a son, and some chroniclers hinted that Lü Buwei was the father and not Zhuang Xiang. The specifics of Ying Zheng's parentage hardly mattered, however, given that the former merchant managed to influence the conduct of the king's reign through his hold over Lady Zhao – and he directed her regency after Zhuang Xiang's death in 247 BCE. Ying Zheng was only a boy, with no alternative but to accept the authority of his mother. As time went on, however, he tired of the tyranny of the Dowager Lady Zhao, whose licentious excesses were threatening the stability of the realm.

Lü Buwei had tired of her too, it seems, and thrown her over as a lover, but provided her with a replacement to appease her rage. Lao Ai, Sima Qian's chronicle soberly reports, had a penis so great in length and girth that it would have made a perfectly adequate axle for a cart. Lü Buwei apparently arranged for this monster of masculinity to undergo a fake castration so that he could be introduced to the Dowager Lady's household as a eunuch. In her appreciation for his skills, Lady Zhao not only bore Lao Ai two children but also bestowed an aristocratic title on him, and allowed him his own retinue of a thousand servants.

Below: The first emperor, Shihuangdi, imagined here by a 19th century Chinese painter, is a picture of ruthlessness and resolve.

The disgrace to the royal house apart, this situation was clearly not one that Ying Zheng (by this time a young man) could be expected to endure. Ordered to leave the palace, Lao Ai turned to the Dowager Lady for help, but in attempting a coup the couple overplayed their hand. Ying Zheng placed his mother under house arrest and had her children by Lao Ai executed. Lao Ai himself was tied by his head, hands and feet to a team of horses, which were then scared into stampeding, bolting off in all directions and tearing him quite literally limb from limb. Sent into exile, Lü Buwei committed suicide by taking poison.

EMPIRE BUILDER

No longer a boy but very much the real ruler of his kingdom, Ying Zheng would no longer be bullied or bamboozled. The official who said he had 'the heart of a tiger' wasn't paying him a compliment, as the full version of his menagerie of metaphors makes clear:

The King of Qin has a wasplike nose; narrow slits for eyes; the breast of a chicken and a voice like a jackal's. He is without mercy: he has the heart of a tiger or a wolf.

Above: Chief among Shihuangdi's concubines, Xi Ling-Shi is traditionally held to have invented the art of growing silkworms and making silk.

Having consolidated his hold over Qin itself, Ying Zheng set about extending his authority, starting in 236 BCE with a two-pronged attack on his state's northeastern neighbour, Zhao. However, his forces became badly bogged down before suffering a serious setback at the Battle of Fei (233 BCE), near Jinzhou, in Hebei province, where the heroic Zhao general Li Mu won a triumphant victory.

Showing the adaptability and unscrupulousness that were to be the hallmarks of his reign, Ying Zheng simply switched his strategy in response. Standing down his forces in Zhao, he sent agents to bribe senior officials in Zhao to whisper to their king that Li Mu was plotting a rebellion against his rule. This plan was ultimately successful, but in the time it took to take effect, Ying Zheng sent troops against Han. A smaller state to the southeast of Qin, Han had already been weakened in successive campaigns by Ying Zheng's late father. After one last big push it fell to Ying Zheng's forces in 230 BCE. Meanwhile, back in Zhao, Li Mu's position had become precarious – as had that of this great kingdom as a whole.

The devastation caused by a terrible earthquake in 229 BCE, and the ravages of the famine that had followed it, left what had seemed an insuperable adversary broken and reeling. In 228 BCE, on hearing that Li Mu had at last been removed from office, Ying Zheng attacked the stricken state. It took seven months' fierce fighting, but at last the Zhao capital, Handan (Hebei province), fell. Ying Zheng's empire was one kingdom bigger and had one fewer foe.

BRUTE FARCE

In 227 BCE, the Crown Prince of Yan (a northeastern coastal state) sent his agent, Jing Ke, to assassinate Ying Zheng with the support of an assistant, Qin Wuyang.

They also had the help of Fan Wuji, a rebel general who had sought sanctuary in Yan, and accordingly had a massive bounty on his head. So resentful was he of his former master that he offered to commit suicide so that the assassins could quite literally carry his head with them into Qin on the pretext that they were coming to claim this reward.

All went according to plan, and the pair were welcomed to Ying Zheng's court at Xianyang. With Qin Wuyang beside him bearing Fan Wuji's bleeding head, Jing Ke approached the king with a poisoned dagger, hidden in a scroll. He was so nervous, however, that he botched his attack, missing with his thrust when the moment came. By protocol, Ying Zheng's courtiers were not armed, so could do little to assist their master in the undignified brawl that followed. Although Qin Wuyang was quickly tackled, Jing Ke remained free and went for the king who, in all the panic and confusion, could not quickly draw his long and unwieldy ceremonial sword.

Finally, the royal physician threw his bag at the assassin, causing him to trip and fall. Although Jing Ke hurled his dagger at the king, he missed, and Ying Zheng was at last able to withdraw his sword from its scabbard and attack Jing Ke, running him through with it eight times in all. He now had the excuse he needed for a full-scale attack on Yan.

THE CONQUEST COMPLETED

Wei was to fall in 225 BCE. Fierce resistance had been extinguished here when General Wang Ben set his men to work for three months digging channels and throwing up embankments to divert the Yellow River on to its capital, Daliang (now Kaifeng, Henan). More than 100,000 people are said to have drowned in the floods that followed – many of them, inevitably, civilians – but this hardly mattered: Ying Zheng had his Wei.

In 223 BCE, after a bitter, two-year campaign, the great kingdom of Chu, to the east, was taken. Next, in 222 BCE, came its northerly neighbour, the little state of Qi. By 221 BCE, Ying Zheng was in a position to formalize the unification of all

Below: A horse-drawn carriage fit for an emperor – part of Shihuangdi's 'Terracotta Army'. In real life, the First Emperor made extensive tours of his domains.

these former kingdoms into a single gigantic state. The China that he had created was something more than its component parts. All told, it covered an area of 2,300,000 sq km (890,000 sq miles). He also bestowed upon himself the title of Shihuangdi. While the *shi* element of this new name merely meant 'the first', and *huang* meant 'glorious', the final di was quite a claim, for it meant 'divine'.

How far was Shihuangdi a tyrant and how far a tough, no-nonsense emperor who got things done? The question can have different answers and – at different times, from different historians, from different backgrounds – has had them both. Much of what the First Emperor did appears in hindsight to have been the impressively efficient fashioning of a major modernizing power out of a self-defeatingly quarrelsome hotch-potch of rival states.

HOW FAR WAS SHIHUANGDI A TYRANT AND HOW FAR A TOUGH, NO-NONSENSE EMPEROR WHO GOT THINGS DONE?

Shihuangdi's first priority was to take complete possession of his empire, in all its isolated corners, disarming local warlords and subjecting them to his own officials. The nobility in the regions were rounded up and brought to live in Xianyang, where they could be closely supervised. He organized his realms into 36 provinces, each overseen by his bureaucracy. A network of new roads assured easy and efficient communications. But Shihuangdi's centralizing drive extended far beyond the normal sphere of government into everything from weights and measures to law and language.

SLAVES OF THE STATE

Were Shihuangdi's people happy? That is perhaps the last question anyone in the ancient world would have thought of asking. To what extent it is answerable now must be doubtful. The peasantry – that is, the overwhelming majority of the population – in every early society led lives of scarcity, unremitting toil and routine oppression. Shihuangdi's people were no exception. If anything, their plight appears to have been somewhat worse, so heavily were they taxed – both in labour and in produce.

It is estimated that the average household had to hand over a full half of the rice, millet or other grain it grew each year, while all males from the ages of 15 to 60 were subject to set periods of corvée – unpaid labour for the state – each year. This included road building and mending; digging dykes and raising and repairing embankments; and work on construction projects, from administrative offices to imperial palaces and tombs. All this was in addition to their military service. That this kind of forced labour was also to be the cornerstone of the empire's notoriously harsh penal system cannot have helped: if such work was a punishment, poverty was clearly a crime.

Did the Chinese peasantry feel pride at the sense that they were the subjects of an up-and-coming empire? If they did, it is clear that few of the privileges trickled down.

A SYSTEM OF INJUSTICE

The Confucian system may have insisted on the acceptance of authority and on loyal service, but it also placed a responsibility of benevolence upon the ruler. With its accent on obedience, its ideal society was to be built on a basis of consent, all classes working together for a common good. A certain universal underlying goodwill was taken as read. But Shihuangdi and his staff did not believe that any such benignity existed: give his subjects an inch, and they would take a mile, they reasoned.

'A state,' said Han Fei (280–233 BCE), Shihuangdi's boyhood tutor and in adulthood his closest adviser, 'has no more than ten people who can be relied on to do good of their own accord. Make it so that people cannot actually do wrong, and the entire community will be kept peaceful.'

The sort of obedience Confucius called for could not be left to chance, in other words. Structures had to be set in place that would make disobedience inconceivable. This philosophy was to become known as 'Legalism'. While in theory it elevated the law to the summit of the social order, in practice it made it an instrument of oppression.

The people were to be kept in line with draconian punishments for even the least transgression. In addition to sentences of forced labour and exile (often, in practice, they went together), the emperor's magistrates were lavish with other punishments: beatings, facial mutilations and tattooings, amputations of hands and feet, castrations. Then, for crimes of treason against Shihuangdi or his state, there was death.

Perhaps it is the privilege that most educated people in the advanced industrialized societies have enjoyed that has allowed us to dismiss the human cost of such a system in hard labour and harsh punishments so lightly. Modern scholarship has generally been more struck by the First Emperor's eagerness to police his people's minds – and there is no doubt that this was sinister.

Shihuangdi distrusted an intellectual as much as he did any foreign raider.

Confucian scholars were no exception. He had 'books' (strictly speaking, scrolls of silk) burned in their thousands at public ceremonies in 213 BCE. He did not destroy texts of practical application in medicine or agriculture, historian Frances Wood points out, but took particular exception to the historical records of the various different 'Warring States' of the preceding era. Like later despots, he sought to erase the sense of any past – and consequently any precedent for arranging things in any other way – in his country's consciousness. He hoped to make the start of his own reign a sort of 'Year Zero'.

Above: As his fellows are bundled into an open grave, one scholar pleads for his life. Shihuangdi saw liberal education as a threat.

In 214 BCE, Shihuangdi took a more radical step towards limiting what could be written and thought within his empire when he had 460 scholars buried alive at a special ceremony.

THE GREAT WALL

JUST AS HE HAD woven China's disunited states into a coherent whole, Shihuangdi joined their scattered fortifications into a single system. Begun on the emperor's orders by General Meng Tian, to protect the gains made in a successful campaign against steppe nomads in 215 BCE, this 'Great Wall of China' ran for 5000km (3000 miles) along the empire's northern frontier.

Awe-inspiring as it was in its vision and engineering, the wall was as much a statement as a construction project. It asserted, in unambiguous and unignorable terms, the integrity of China as its own single, separate state. As important as its military function in excluding China's traditional tormentors, the steppe nomads, may have been, it also served as a symbolic demarcation between Chinese civilization and the (implicitly barbaric) world outside.

Shihuangdi was not the first Chinese monarch to build a frontier wall; nor does much of his 2200-year-old construction survive (traces have been identified in Shanxi, Gansu, Hebei and Liaoning provinces). It is possible that he built 'his' wall in the same way as he had his empire: atop the foundations and surviving structures of others who had gone before.

Attitudes to this great construction have changed, even in China. For centuries, Shihuangdi's work – and the refurbishments and improvements of his various successors – were seen as evidence of the emperors' tyrannical vainglory, like a sort of Chinese Tower of Babel. It was even, early critics suggested, an assault on the earth, a 'cutting of its arteries'. Well into modern times, scholars were more concerned with the millions who must have died doing forced labour on its construction down the generations than impressed with the extraordinary scale of the achievement.

Below: This modern artist's impression is entirely anachronistic – but it captures Shihuangdi's Great Wall as an expression of his power.

Above: As massively substantial as it was, the Great Wall was also and importantly a metaphor, emblematizing China's coherence as a single state.

POSTHUMOUS POMP

The sort of power and prestige that Shihuangdi enjoyed could not have been easy to relinquish. Even in death, the First Emperor hoped to hold on to his exalted status. Hence the massive size of his burial mound, rising out of the slopes of Mount Li, which itself stands high above the fields of Shaanxi province. Inside, and deep within the mountain, extends a fabulous complex of passages and chambers, at the heart of which the emperor was laid to rest. More than 700,000 prisoners are said to have laboured for several decades to construct this extraordinary earthwork.

More astonishing still, however, have been the treasures uncovered in four pits found some 1.6km (about a mile) away. Here, concealed in wood-roofed vaults, but lined up apparently in defence of their departed commander-in-chief, was an army of life-size terracotta figures 7000 strong. The force includes officers and generals as well as ordinary soldiers, armed with real spears; there are mounted cavalrymen and charioteers as well as crossbowmen. There are also non-combatants, from officials to acrobats. Each is an individual, lovingly sculpted: no two faces are the same, and a wide range of ages, physiques and characters is represented.

BLOODY BURIAL

Archaeological interest has focused on this 'Terracotta Army' – its historical significance, aesthetic significance and its sheer scale. It might also offer an insight into a possible advance in ethical awareness. Shang rulers went to their tombs with sacrificially slaughtered human staff. Could the creation of this artificial army be said to have saved thousands of human lives?

If the Terracotta Army did serve as a ceramic substitute for a comparable number of living, human soldiers, this would obviously be welcome. But many people still seem to have lost their lives in the construction of this funerary complex. Some may have died of natural causes, while many could have lost their lives in accidents in what was probably difficult and dangerous work. Even so, it seems that a sizeable number of people were sacrificed too. Many mass graves have been found on the site, some of which have been excavated, revealing the immolated remains of young women, believed to have been concubines sent to accompany their emperor into the earth. Other grave pits were crammed with male bodies – those of labourers and craftsmen, sent to serve Shihuangdi in the next life. Or perhaps they were killed to ensure their silence, as it is known that the First Emperor feared having his resting place disturbed. Entrance tunnels were said to have been booby-trapped to keep out robbers.

Below: Carried to the workings in his imperial litter, Shihuangdi oversees the construction of the tomb he hoped he'd never actually have to occupy.

Above: If Shihuangdi had to die, he was determined to go into the darkness well-attended and well-protected – hence his 7000-strong 'Terracotta Army'.

IN SEARCH OF IMMORTALITY

However stupendous his tomb, Shihuangdi was in no hurry to occupy it. The fear of death perplexed (perhaps even angered) him from middle age on. He had life-and-death power over so many millions – why couldn't he control his own destiny? Why should so illustrious a personage have to submit to the indignity of death?

That Shihuangdi grew paranoid was not surprising. His rule had been consciously harsh: he had made no pretence of seeking his people's love. Jing Ke's attack of 227 BCE had been followed by a further two assassination attempts – both of them unsuccessful but still frightening. In the first, a 'minstrel' who had come to entertain Shihuangdi swung to hit him with a lead-weighted lute, before being fought off. In the second, a giant solid bronze cone was dropped from a height on to the imperial cavalcade, but crushed the carriage before the emperor's. In any case, Shihuangdi was temperamentally suspicious. At best, he could be characterized as shrewdly sceptical; hence his favouring an abrasive Legalism over Confucius' comparatively upbeat communitarian creed.

Increasingly, however, that scepticism seems to have abandoned Shihuangdi as, in his later decades, he hurled himself into the quest for some supernatural means of extending earthly life. In 219 BCE, he sent several thousand young men and women off on an expedition to find the Island of Immortals, said by tradition to lie somewhere off his country's eastern coast. They were to bring back the special herbs he assumed would be its secret of everlasting life. When this group did not return, the emperor dispatched a smaller expedition a few years later, but they fared better only to the extent of returning to Xianyiang safely. Their way to the island, they claimed, had been barred by a giant fish.

Below: This modern statue of Shihuangdi stands on the lower slopes of Mount Li, in Shaanxi province, but his real monument is his nearby tomb-complex.

DEATH AND DISORDER

Shihuangdi was left with no alternative, he felt, but to set off himself in search of this fabled island and of the enchanted cures it must contain. He was travelling when, in 210 BCE, he fell ill and died. The circumstances are obscure: some chroniclers claimed that he had ironically suffered mercury poisoning from a mixture that he had been taking as an immortality elixir. The courtiers taking him back to Xianyiang – a journey that took many days – were desperate to delay the official announcement of his death. Accordingly, it is said, they had cartloads of rotten fish carried both before and behind his body to mask the smell of his decomposing body.

Just as his retainers had feared, anarchy followed the First Emperor's death. His closest advisers, apparently afraid of now being marginalized, forged evidence that his son Fusu had been plotting to assassinate him. The Crown

Above: By tradition, Liu Bang slew a white serpent which had been poisoning the populace. It turned out to have been the Second Emperor's son.

Prince and his friend General Meng Tian were both forced to commit suicide. However, the younger prince who ended up ascending the throne as Qin Er Shi (Second Emperor) lacked his father's authority, and China quickly descended into disorder.

There are good grounds for suggesting that Shihuangdi's legacy survives in China to this day. Dynastically, though, it was to be short-lived. Qin Er Shi spent his short reign striving to suppress a series of revolts, by supporters of Fusu, by discontented peasants, and by opportunistic local thugs. The emperor's attempts to crack down on this kind of opposition, making an already harsh system still more punitive, only exacerbated the resistance to his rule.

A CHAOTIC SUCCESSION

Noble families in the old autonomous kingdoms began to reassert themselves. The state of Chou rose up against the power of Qin. When in 207 BCE the separatists all but annihilated an imperial army at the Battle of Julu (Pingxiang, Hebei province), Qin Er Shi's authority was left in shreds. The Second Emperor was forced by his ministers to commit suicide; his throne was given to one Ziying.

It is not known what this third emperor's antecedents were – some said that he was a son of Fusu. In any case, the empire began to crash into confusion around his ears even as Xianyiang burned, sacked by one of any number of rebel groups. Ziying's rule ended in December 207 BCE after only 46 days.

As an imperial dynasty, the House of Qin had lasted only fourteen years. The political vacuum it left behind was filled with anarchy as Ziying's killers battled for supremacy with a rival rebel force led by Liu Bang (256–195 BCE). A former imperial policeman of peasant origins, Liu Bang was a charismatic and cunning leader: by 202 BCE, he had claimed the role of emperor. The title he took was Gaozu, and the dynasty he established, the Han, was to dominate Chinese life for 400 years.

LIGHT RELIEF

Gaozu began by breaking with the past, building a new capital, Chang'an (X'ian), only a few kilometres west along the Wei River from Xianyiang. In hindsight this seems fitting, for different as his rhetoric as ruler was, Gaozu would not wander all that far from the imperial agenda as worked out by Shihuangdi. Most of the First Emperor's centralized institutional structures stayed in place, although Gaozu's ruling style was very different.

Below: As the Emperor Gaozu, Liu Bang makes his processional entrance into the new imperial capital he had constructed at Chang'an.

By temperament, he was much more emollient: laws were applied more leniently, censorship relaxed, and the civil service allowed more autonomy.

Where Shihuangdi had been highly visible and hands-on, Gaozu was content to withdraw into the background. His policy of handing out local kingships to family members in the regions might be storing up trouble for the future, but it helped to ensure the smooth running of the empire in the immediate term. Gaozu's bureaucrats became the dominant class in China. So conscientious, well trained and organized were they that this was no bad thing.

Below: Gaozu never forgot his peasant origins, modelling a whole district of his new capital, Chang'an, on his birthplace, Feng, in Chu, in central China.

The only real shadow hanging over Gaozu's China at this time was the menace represented by yet another steppe nomad people: the Xiongnu. Forebears of the Huns who a few centuries later would terrorize Roman Europe, they had been taking advantage of the recent chaos to terrorize China. Gaozu, not yet ready to fight them, tried to buy them off with tribute, even sending a princess to marry the Xiongnu leader. Surprisingly, perhaps, the policy appears to have worked.

DARK DOWAGER

After Gaozu's death in battle in 195 BCE, his widow, the Dowager Empress Lü, held sway as regent. For the chroniclers, she is a hate figure, alleged to have schemed and murdered to assure her son and grandson's succession over those of the emperor's other wives and concubines, and to have placed her own relations in key positions. Her eldest son Hui (210–188 BCE) was weak, though by all accounts honourable and decent. Gaozu was known to have favoured another son for the succession: Liu Ruyi (208–194 BCE), born to him by his favourite concubine, Qi.

Below: Gaozu's widow Lü proved a potent – and often cruel – Dowager Empress.

Fearful of his mother's motives, the young Emperor Hui tried to protect his half-brother, it is said, and successfully saw off several attempts at murder on her part. In the end, however, Lü saw her opportunity when Hui went off on a hunting trip one day. The Dowager had her men take Liu Ruyi and force-feed him poison until he died. Seizing his helpless mother, Qi, they cut off her limbs, gouged out her eyes, cut off her nose and ears and then finally cut out her tongue. They threw the bleeding head and torso into a pigsty – fit punishment for one the Dowager said was a 'human swine'. Only some days after this did Hui, his suspicions rising, order a search for her. His horror at the state in which she was found prompted something like a nervous breakdown in him. He lost interest in his office and gave himself up to debauchery and drink.

Hui's son Qianshao (193–184 BCE) had also been born to a concubine. She in turn had been cruelly killed by the Dowager Empress, who maintained that she herself was Qianshao's mother – and that the late Emperor Gaozu had fathered him as one of his last acts. The boy was brought up believing this, we are told. When he eventually found out the truth and warned that Lü and her supporters would be brought to justice, she had Qianshao imprisoned, announcing that he was being nursed through a severe mental illness. Backed by her retainers, she had him pronounced insane, deposed and discreetly executed.

Qianshao's brother Liu Yin (190–180 BCE), as the Emperor Houshao, succeeded him. Aged six when he ascended the throne, he could only have been a puppet of the Dowager Empress, and when she died in 180 BCE he was in no position to defend himself. His uncle, Liu Heng (202–157 BCE), one of Emperor Gaozu's surviving younger sons (his mother had been the concubine Bo), won out in the inevitable succession struggle.

SHE HAD HIM PRONOUNCED INSANE, DEPOSED AND DISCREETLY EXECUTED.

FROM WEN TO WU

As the Emperor Wen, Liu Heng appears to have reigned well. So too, for the most part, did his successor Jing, who was emperor from 157 to 141 BCE. Jing's attempts to centralize his kingdom further, Shihuangdi-style, were impeded first by a jealous younger brother and then by the various cousins – local kings – who in 154 BCE staged the Rebellion of the Seven States. Jing saw off these challenges and was succeeded by his 15-year-old son Wu (157–87 BCE). His reign was to last for 54 years.

Wu's reign was largely quiet – for him at least, albeit not for those southern peoples he sent his conquering armies against, making important territorial gains, including some in Myanmar and Vietnam.

In his dealings with the Xiongnu nomads on the northern steppe, Wu was to drop the policy of appeasement pursued by Gaozu and his successors in favour of a much more aggressive approach. An eight-year campaign drove the Xiongnu north and westward. In 133 BCE, an army led by Wei Qing, a kinsman of the emperor, struck deep into the Gobi desert and, at the Battle of

Above: This particular expedition against the Xiongnu (99 BCE), didn't work out well for Wu. General Ling Li was defeated, and defected to the Huns.

Mobei, scored a shattering victory over the Xiongnu. The costs for Han China had been enormous, but the nomads had suffered worse, losing tens of thousands of warriors and vast areas of territory. With garrisons installed and regular patrols inaugurated to protect them, more than 100,000 colonists were established in what had been the frontier zone. Wu sent further armies north into Korea and Manchuria.

China's victories over the nomads had not only brought greater security, but also had opened up access to that great overland trade route known as the Silk Road. Almost 1500 years before Marco Polo described his journey to China along

Above: More stylized – and more 'coinlike' – than the knives exchanged in earlier times, this currency was introduced by Wang Mang.

this route, Wu's ambassador, Chiang Chien, travelled much of it in the opposite direction. The purpose of his journey was not commercial but diplomatic: he hoped to establish alliances against the Xiongnu with tribes in Bactria, northern Afghanistan.

Chiang Chien did not succeed, but he did open Chinese eyes, as well as opening up economic opportunities that would eventually prove immense. Over the decades that followed, under successive emperors, China's hold on eastern sections of the Silk Road was consolidated. The oasis towns of the Tarim Basin were taken as a base for the camel caravans now plying what was becoming an important commercial artery. Links were established with Roman settlements in Parthia and beyond, although there does not seem to have been any direct contact between these two great empires.

COUNTING THE COST

Despite the advantages in increased trade and agricultural productivity, the costs of this expansionism were becoming crippling. The scale of Han China's imperial enterprise was vast; the expenses were correspondingly enormous. To give just one example: in 119 BCE alone, the records show, 100,000 army horses had to be replaced. The tax burden on the people grew steadily heavier.

Despite territorial gains, China was running out of cultivable land, the population having grown so quickly during the decades of prosperity. With so many peasants left landless, there was an inevitable upturn in agrarian unrest; this smouldered on, with occasional flare-ups, through the first century. Big landowners were emboldened to defy officials and withhold their taxes, compounding the chaos. In 9 CE, the adviser Wang Mang (c. 45 BCE–23 CE), who had been appointed regent over a one-year-old supposed emperor, saw a chance to seize power for himself. He announced that he was establishing his own dynasty, the Xin.

Sensing, like Shihuangdi and Jing before him, that the nobility in the regions were growing too wayward, Wang Mang made strenuous efforts to break their power. But everything seemed to conspire against him – not least his own temperament. Quiet and scholarly as he was, he may have been touched by arrogance (and was certainly too ambitious by half), but he really wasn't cut out for tyranny. A bad bout of flooding in 11 CE washed away the year's rice harvest and a severe famine followed, and Wang Mang found himself an enemy not just of the aristocrats but of the peasantry. His forces struggled to suppress a revolt by the 'Red Eyebrows' (so-called because adherents of the movement literally painted their eyebrows red as a mark of membership). As the state sank into anarchy, a growing range of rebel groups included a faction supporting Liu Hsiu, a descendant of the Han.

Above: This representation of Guangwu was one of a series of imperial portraits created by the Tang court painter Yan Liben in the seventh century.

In 23 CE, a rebel army seized Chang'an. They stormed the imperial palace and killed Wang Mang. With him ended the Xin Dynasty – although it had hardly been a 'dynasty' at all, given that Wang Mang had ended up its only member. Two years later, Liu Hsiu was able to pronounce himself emperor. He would reign under the name Guangwu, of the House of Han.

NEW DYNASTY, OLD PROBLEMS

Guangwu wanted the prestige of leading a restored Han China, but he did not want it dragged down by the difficulties that

THE YELLOW RIVER

When the Chinese wanted the ultimate example of something they did not expect to happen in anybody's lifetime, they said it would happen 'when Huang He runs clear,' the Jesuit missionary Matteo Ricci (1552–1610) noted. The 'Yellow River' takes its name from the colour of its waters, which are clogged with mud. The reason it is so thick with silt is that the part of north-central China across which it chiefly runs, the Huangtu Plateau, is composed of loess – sedimentary deposits ground to powdery fineness through successive glaciations, then blown by the wind. It could hardly be more erodible, flaking away at the lightest touch.

Like other rivers, the Yellow River is prone to seasonal flooding. Every spring, the snowmelt in the mountains brings another surge downstream and the Huang He is liable to burst its banks. Again, this is by no means unusual – nor, in itself, an especially bad thing. Agriculture in the world's river floodplains relies on this regular replenishment of their soils. Here, however, the consequences are much less predictable and more dangerous. The friability of the rock means that, every time the Yellow River rises, the bluffs, cliffs and other landforms along its route are liable to be washed away. The same goes for the embankments and barriers built by farming communities to contain the flow. The river can quite abruptly change its course.

Sometimes this happens radically, and with catastrophic consequences for the communities in its vicinity. One disaster of the 14th century claimed more than seven million lives. Another in the 1880s killed almost a million. As we have seen, a disastrous flood had hit the region around the start of the second millennium BCE: Yu had established the legitimacy of the Xia Dynasty by his work to protect the people. With a little help from Wang Ben, the Yellow River had played a part in the history of the Han Dynasty. The floods of 11 CE are said to have cut short the sway of Wang Mang's Xin Dynasty.

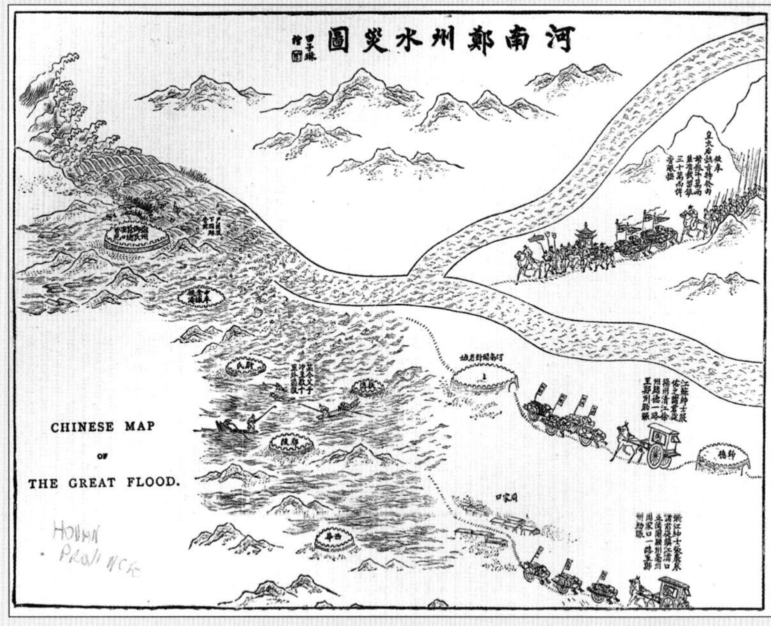

had dogged its dying decades. In token of the fresh start he was making, he transferred his headquarters to the old Eastern Zhou capital at Luoyang.

Guangwu's Western Han dynasty was to reign for almost 200 years. It cannot be characterized as a failure, but neither was it a real success. Its achievements do not compare with those of the Eastern Han, whose economic problems had not been significantly addressed. The peasantry were just as hungry and just as unhappy as they had been before. The nobility, meanwhile, were just as wayward, and in the face of their uncooperativeness, successive emperors found themselves more or less at the mercy of their own advisers.

THE PEASANTRY WERE JUST AS HUNGRY AND UNHAPPY AS THEY HAD BEEN BEFORE.

The second century saw this chronic crisis deepen: the 'ruling' dynasty was becoming an irrelevance. Agrarian unrest was simmering across the empire. The continuing cost of protecting territories and trading posts along the Silk Road was being borne by an already struggling Chinese peasantry for whom this frontier enterprise seemed – both geographically and imaginatively – impossibly remote. The swelling of their ranks by returning colonists, discouraged by droughts and famines in these northern realms, only exacerbated these difficulties. That the great landowners saw this over-supply of labour as an opportunity for profiteering brought existing resentments to boiling point.

A DYNASTY DISINTEGRATES

In 184 CE, the 'Yellow Turbans', a hitherto marginal Taoist sect, rose in rebellion in the northeasterly Shandong province. They wrapped their heads with yellow scarves to advertise their allegiance – hence the rising's name. It was to galvanize peasants across the empire.

The unrest was suppressed, but at enormous human cost: an estimated 100,000 rebels were killed. The political price was high as well; the Han regime's reliance on leading aristocrats in the regions to help put down the insurrections had left them sadly short of authority over what were now powerful and well-armed warlords.

Again, the Han prevailed, thanks to the brutal effectiveness of the imperial general Cao Cao (c. 155–220 CE), but once again they had to pay a fearful price. First, they were forced to surrender a considerable area of territory south of the Yangtze River, which Cao Cao had been unable to take back from local warlords Sun Quan (182–252 CE) and Liu Bei (161–223 CE). Second, once the dust had cleared, they found themselves dependent on the military strongman who had saved them. He became the real power behind the throne. Even that eminence was not sufficient for Cao Cao's son Cao Pi (c. 187–226 CE), who on his father's death seized power himself. His coup called time on the Han Dynasty once and for all.

OUTMANOEUVRED

Cao Cao was to pass into Chinese history as a hero, illustrious for both his courage and his cunning. But he met his match in 208 CE in Liu Bei and Sun Quan, who sent his imperial forces packing at the Battle of Red Cliffs. The two southern warlords, allied for the occasion, had treated Cao Cao's warnings to surrender with contempt. The imperial chancellor might (as he maintained) have 800,000 men at his command, but they were confident that their combined force of 70,000 would win them victory.

Much of Cao Cao's force had sailed upriver in a fleet of ships, which came to anchor in a gorge beneath the 'Red Cliffs' of the battle's name. This little navy should have added an extra dimension to his attack. In the event, his peasant soldiers were so spooked at being afloat on the Yangtze's choppy waters that they were reduced to helplessness – and Cao Cao had to chain all the vessels together into a block. Sun Quan's general Huang Gai is said to have hit on the idea of sending Cao Cao a letter pretending that he had fallen out with his overlord and was coming over to his side; he was going to cross the river with his men aboard a flotilla of ships, he said. The rebels loaded their vessels with straw, dry sticks and casks of oil, which, just as they neared the imperial ships, they set on fire before abandoning.

Chained together as they were, Cao Cao's ships were unable to take evasive action. The imperial force fled for the shore in confusion and scattered, panic-stricken. The rebel foot soldiers had closed and exacted severe casualties by the time Cao Cao succeeded in calling his men to some kind of order. His only option was to give the command for a retreat.

This was also the end, for the time being, of China itself as a single state. The Han Empire broke up into three separate kingdoms, as, still unvanquished, the kingdoms controlled by Sun Quan and Liu Bei broke free. Unsurprisingly, these warlords saw no reason why they should submit to joining the imperial rump led by the kingdom Cao Wei. Liu Bei's territories became Shu Han (in token of his claim to be the true heir to the empire of the Han), while Sun Quan's state became its own 'empire': Wu.

The main purpose of these states seems to have been to go to war with one another. This 'Three Kingdoms' period was arguably the bloodiest in Chinese history – much more

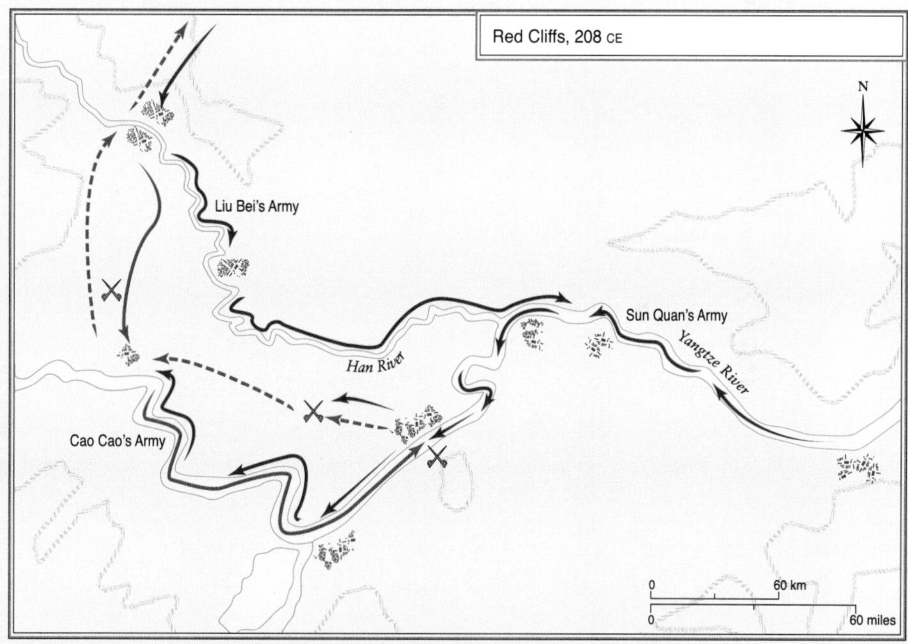

Right: Map showing the course of Battle of Red Cliffs.

Unfortunately, their journey – now on foot – took them squelching slowly and painfully across some of the boggiest terrain in China, making them an easy target for rebel archers and skirmishing parties.

That the Battle of Red Cliffs really took place is not seriously disputed, although its precise location is debated to this day. Along with its historical importance, moreover, it has taken on mythohistorical significance in Chinese folk memory as an example of cunning and resourcefulness winning out over strength.

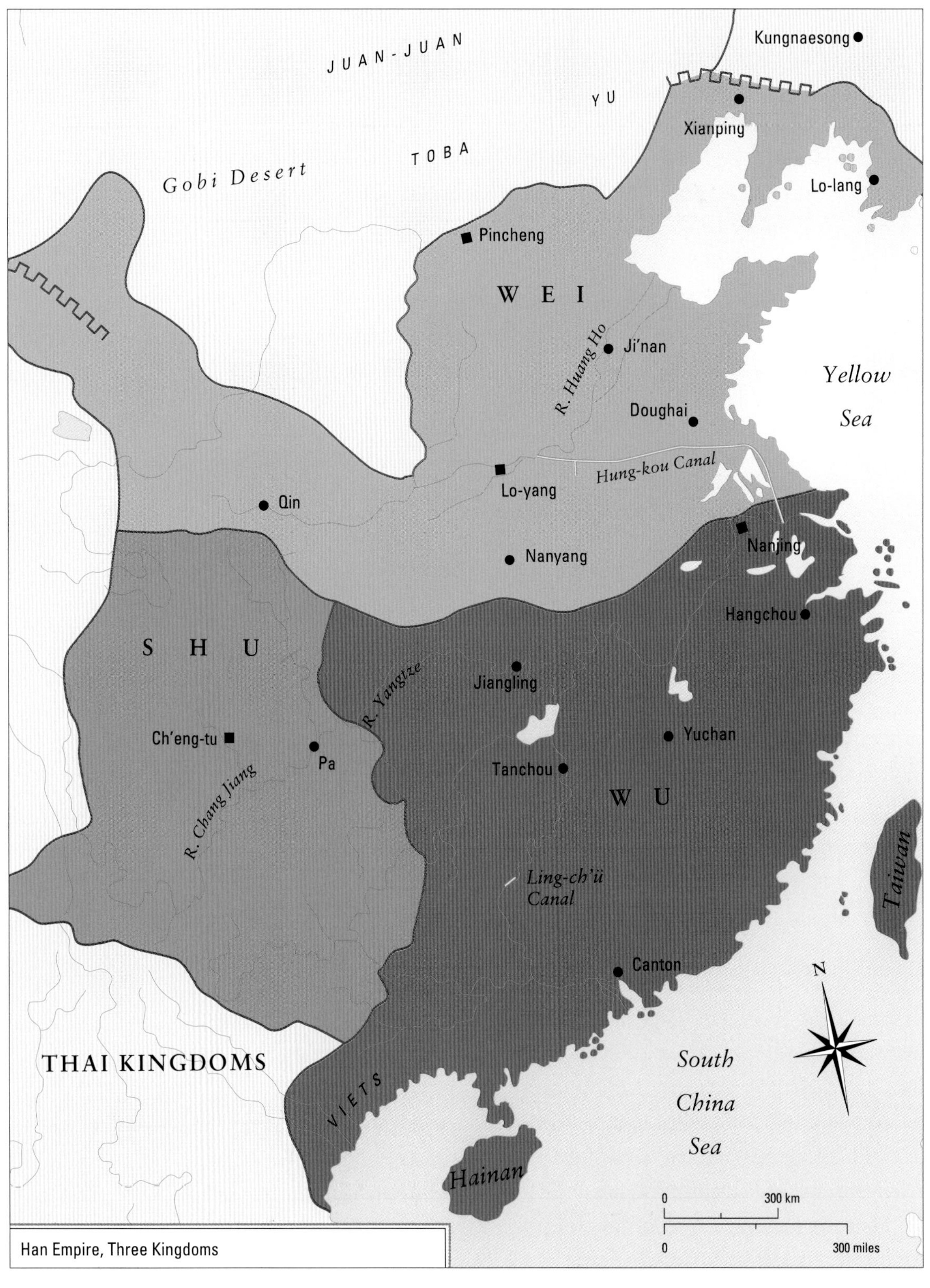

Han Empire, Three Kingdoms

so than the age of the 'Warring States'. It did not go on for long – sixty years or so – but was a living nightmare while it lasted. An official census at the end of the Han era had recorded the population of the empire as over 56 million. By the time Emperor Wu (236–290 CE) came to take the next count soon after establishing his Jin Dynasty in 280 CE, it had fallen to less than 17 million.

Opposite: Seeing the Three Kingdoms mapped out like this is essential for clarity's sake, though the impression of civility and order it produces is most misleading.

JEALOUS JIA

The order that the Jin Dynasty restored was extremely welcome to China, but it did not extend to the very top – certainly not in the decade from 290 CE when Jia Nanfeng (257–300 CE), the Empress Jia, was making herself the real, murderous and dictatorial, power in the realm. She had been characterized by her future father-in-law Wu as 'jealous, ugly, short and dark-skinned' and the record would seem to confirm at least the first of these descriptors. Even so, Wu had been persuaded to accept her as a bride for his son, the Crown Prince Sima Zhong (259–307 CE).

[EMPRESS JIA] HAD BEEN CHARACTERIZED BY HER FUTURE FATHER-IN-LAW WU AS 'JEALOUS, UGLY, SHORT AND DARK-SKINNED'.

The prince's mental and physical disabilities seemed to call for an unusually strong, intelligent and understanding wife. As his father had perhaps anticipated, the advent of his reign as the Emperor Hui was the signal for the empire's nobles to start jostling for control. The Empress Jia saw off all these threats, but turned out to represent a menace all her own.

To begin with, the cautious checks set in place by her father-in-law limited Jia's power over Emperor Hui – the Dowager Empress Yang (259–292 CE) and her father, a senior minister, Yang Jun, were named as regents. But Jia conspired with courtiers and princes to have Yang Jun denounced as a traitor. Despite his attempts to defend himself by military force – he sent an army to besiege the royal palace – he was defeated.

Now it was easy enough for Jia to take similar action against the Dowager Empress. She was imprisoned, leaving the field clear for Empress Jia. Even now, however, Jia was underestimated: leading nobles sought to oust her, only to find themselves quickly vanquished and put to death.

Jia's authority was now unquestioned. She had achieved what she had set out to do. Was it for this reason that she now started to fall apart? The controlled, controlling manner slipped and she became a woman possessed by dark and untrammelled passions – largely sexual (she was rampantly adulterous), but jealous too. She had many of her lovers murdered – partly, perhaps, so they could not 'kiss and tell', but also, it seems, so that others couldn't also possess them.

SHE BECAME A WOMAN POSSESSED BY DARK AND UNTRAMMELLED PASSIONS.

Crown Prince Sima Yu (278–300 CE) had been born to Emperor Wu by a concubine, so had not been seen as a likely candidate for emperor – or, consequently, regarded by Jia as a threat. Now, however, as she sensed her own counsellors growing uneasy at her volatility and violence, she came to feel that they were looking Yu's way. Summoning him to her presence one day, she had him plied with wine, then made him write out a 'confession' admitting to a plot to assassinate the Emperor Hui and herself.

SUCCESSION STRUGGLES

Yu was duly deposed from his position, but this was not enough for Empress Jia; she now sent assassins to murder him. Her advisers, deciding that enough was enough, turned on her and had her deposed. She was forced to kill herself by drinking wine with gold fragments in it. The so-called 'War of the Eight Princes' over Hui's regency had arguably been under way since his accession in 290 CE, but Jia had been a strong and ruthless presence at the emperor's side. Now, however, with Jia gone, the conflict got going in earnest.

Not till 307 CE did one prince, Sima Yue, a cousin of Emperor Wu, come out on top. This left him ideally placed to act as regent to Hui's successor when that unfortunate emperor died – he had been poisoned, seemingly by Sima Yue himself. But Huai (284–313 CE), another young son of the Jin Dynasty's founding emperor Wu, was formidably intelligent and tough, and did not need a regent for long. He allied himself with a leading general and together they marginalized the overbearing Sima Yue, who died in despair in 311 CE.

Huai did not get to triumph for long, however: Liu Cong, the leader of the Xiongnu state of Han Zhao, had taken advantage of the empire's disunity to encroach on China from the north. In 311 CE, he captured Luoyang and took the emperor hostage. Liu Cong had Huai poisoned in 313 CE. Liu Cong was also to execute Huai's successor, Emperor Min (300–318 CE).

There was no doubt that the Xiongnu were back as a force to be reckoned with in Chinese affairs, but they were just one of several peoples who were taking advantage of the empire's weakness at this time. The so-called 'Five Barbarians' included, along with the Xiongnu, another nation of steppe nomads, the Mongolian Xianbei. Both invaded the northern provinces of the empire, along with another agrarian people, the Jie. Meanwhile, western China was settled by tribes who came down from the adjacent uplands: the Di, a farming people, and the pastoralist Qiang.

The 'Five Barbarians' were divided among themselves, which is why, within a generation or so of their arrival, China entered what has become known as its 'Sixteen Kingdoms' era. Warring statelets rose and fell almost too quickly to be chronicled. The Eastern Jin Dynasty, whose capital was at Jiankang (Nanjing in what is now Jiangsu province), endured for another century, but its territories were much reduced.

Below: An unimpressed-looking Liu Cong receives the submission of two errant ministers in a painting dating from the 15th century.

TARSSIA
REY DEL TAURIS
LO REY DE LILI
ARABIA SABBA

3

Accomplished in Cruelty

Astonishing achievement, the highest civilization, but all at the most terrible human cost: that was the paradox of medieval China.

Visiting Jining, Shandong, towards the end of the 13th century, the Venetian traveller Marco Polo (1254–1324) marvelled at the 'staggering' volume of its water traffic. 'This city has such grand ships,' he said, 'such a large quantity of vessels, that no one could believe it if they hadn't seen it.' The suggestion that Polo might not have seen it either does not undermine testimony that was corroborated by other travellers of the time.

The amount of freight moved up and down through Jining was truly wondrous. The city owed its bustling trade to its situation on the north bank of the Grand Canal, around the halfway mark in its course between Beijing and Hangzhou (Zhejiang province). Many thousands in the city worked on the canal itself or in associated transport jobs; tens of thousands more were employed in port-based industries.

More than 1750km (1100 miles) long, this great waterway joined the Yellow River with the Yangtze and provided a safe

Opposite: China, as it appeared in the pages of the *Catalan Atlas*, created for King Charles V of France in 1375.

commercial corridor through the heart of the Chinese emperor's realms. By optimizing communication and facilitating the movement of troops and military supplies, moreover, it enhanced the authorities' ability to keep control. Although sections, linking local centres, dated back to the first millennium BCE, they had been enlarged, improved and joined together during the Sui Dynasty (581–618). The 'Grand Canal' is generally viewed as dating back to then.

The canal's completion was seen as the culminating achievement of the reign of Emperor Yangdi (569–618) – and it was an impressive accomplishment by any standards. However, it was one for which China's people had paid an appalling price. Like so many projects since the time of Shihuangdi, the Grand Canal had been constructed by corvéed labour – not just its channels but all its bridges, locks and watchhouses. Every inch of rock and earth had been painstakingly cut away by hand. Every building stone had been brought in, carefully shaped and hauled into place by conscripted labour. Millions had been pressed into this gruelling, dirty and often dangerous work through the Sui period – and fewer than fifty per cent are believed to have survived their service.

Below: The construction of the Grand Canal was to transform China's economic fortunes – but the costs, in life and labour, were immense.

ORDER RESTORED

China had struggled to survive the turmoil of the Sixteen Kingdoms period, but what hadn't quite killed the country had seemingly made it strong. It had settled down into something like stability in the era of the Northern and Southern Dynasties.

Things were still as volatile as ever at the top of society: ruling houses rose quickly out of nowhere and were as abruptly overthrown. However, as experienced by China as a whole, this was a time of comparative order. The ruling elites in these new states had been radically 'sinicized' – enthusiastically adopting Chinese ways. In bureaucracy, law and social order, they were on their way to overall conformity even before, in 581, the Emperor Wen (541–604) took the whole empire back under actual Chinese rule.

Order, like charity, begins at home, Wen might have reflected ruefully between his spasms of pain as he lay dying. He had been poisoned by his second son, Yang Guang, it was generally believed. His father duly dispatched, Yang Guang went on to have his elder brother Yang Yong assassinated and to seize the throne himself as the Yangdi emperor. His rule was in its turn contested by another brother, Yiang Liang. With the support of leading generals, Yiang Liang raised a significant rebellion against Yangdi, but the emperor successfully put this down.

Above: Wen brought the entire empire back under Chinese rule in 581, fitting him for inclusion with Yan Liben's Thirteen Emperors.

SUCCESS OF SORTS

Yangdi went on to conduct a most successful reign – successful by certain measures at least. It was Yangdi who completed the Grand Canal. He also built a great deal of the Great Wall of China as we currently know it, refurbishing and rebuilding Shihuangdi's earlier construction. Again, though, there were considerable costs to be borne – and not just in expense and labour but in life. In addition to an estimated 1.5 million labourers killed in the construction of the Grand Canal, some six million were said to have died while working on the Wall. To all these losses have to be added the unknown number who succumbed to malaria in the course of an expedition into Champa (now central and southern Vietnam) – another 'success' that was to be very costly in casualties.

Yangdi's campaigns against Koguryo, a kingdom in the north of Korea, between 598 and 614, could not be characterized as successful in any way, however. China's losses numbered in the hundreds of thousands, and for no meaningful strategic return. Soon the empire was rising up against Yangdi.

Below: The Battle of Salsu (612) brought defeat for China against the Korean kingdom of Koguryo. The Emperor Yangdi was never really to live it down.

In 617, a military coup was mounted against Yangdi. Having been sent out to crush the rebels, his general, Li Yuan (566–635), had become their leader. He now marched his army to the imperial palace and took Yangdi prisoner, replacing him with Yangdi's young grandson, Yang You (605–19). The boy was obviously just a puppet: Li Yuan was actually in charge in China, though nominally at least the Sui Dynasty was still in power. But Yangdi knew this was the end and, finally, in April 618, he asked for the opportunity to commit suicide. His persecutors agreed to bring him poison. Since none could be found, the sometime emperor pleaded with those who had humiliated him to have pity and dispatch him. One of his officers obliged, strangling him with his scarf.

Above: One of the self-mythologizing stories Li Yuan wove around himself was that he had won his wife in an archery contest.

Within a few months, Yang You had handed his throne over to Li Yuan, who set about ruling as Gaozu, first emperor of the Tang Dynasty. Few chroniclers were convinced that Yang You's death a few weeks later was coincidental, although there is no direct evidence that Gaozu or his henchmen were involved.

TOUGH AT THE TOP

'Uneasy lies the head that wears a crown,' said Shakespeare's Henry IV. Successive Chinese emperors were certainly to find this. In 604, Yangdi had clambered over the bodies of his father and

DESTINY AND CHANCE

In 605, a soothsayer's warning prompted Yangdi to leave Chang'an for a secondary capital at Luoyang (the old capital of the Eastern Zhou). Such were the quirks by which China's historic destiny has sometimes been decided. Luoyang's development did also make sense in the context of Yangdi's wider economic plans (including the Grand Canal, on whose banks it stood). And the transition was certainly successful – so much so that the new Luoyang was soon the empire's second-largest city. But the diviner's message had been key.

Divination had been influential in Chinese civilization since the earliest times. The future was read in the random patterning to be found on animal entrails or tortoiseshells, or by counting up cast cowrie shells or plant stalks (later coins). These, or other analogous methods, are by no means unique to China; they were used by ancient civilizations across Asia, Africa, Europe and the Americas as well. But their use continued in the East for a great deal longer than it did elsewhere. Over time, moreover, they had been supplemented by more sophisticated astrological methods; diviners also learned to read clients' futures in their faces (their proportions and their lines) and their palms. Kau cim – the pulling of numbered sticks from a bamboo cylinder – is believed to date from around the sixth century.

The 'Fortune Cookie' served up in Chinese restaurants in the West in modern times may be just a bit of fun, but comparable customs have been taken very seriously in China.

elder brother to attain the throne. Now, in 626, Gaozu's younger son, Li Shimin (598–649), killed his elder brothers and their sons before compelling his father to step down. Li Shimin seized his imperial office and reigned as Emperor Taizong.

As if to offset the crimes he had committed on his path to power, Taizong conducted himself more or less blamelessly. In his later years, however, he suffered from ill health. But, while his nine sons and their supporters bitterly contested his succession, the struggle was inconclusive. When he died in 649 the imperial title went – as he had wished – to his Crown Prince Li Zhi (628–83), who reigned as Emperor Gaozong.

Opposite: Chinese fortune-tellers of the early 20th century.

HER FACE HER FORTUNE

Wu Zhao (624–705) had first come to court as a concubine for Taizong. She had got to know Crown Prince Li Zhi when both had attended his father's deathbed. As emperor, Gaozong gave Wu Zhao a promotion, and the poetic-sounding title 'Lady of Luminous Demeanour'. As one of Gaozong's foremost concubines, Wu Zhao was now effectively in competition with the existing empress, Wang Yu (628–55). Gaozong's wife was proving infertile, while Wu bore him a series of sons.

Below: Taizong receives an envoy from Tibet. The Tang emperor had scored a succession of triumphs over China's enemies.

She also bore a daughter. This child was found a few days later, strangled – murdered by Wang, Wu maintained, in a jealous rage. Many at the court muttered that Wu had actually killed her own child (a daughter, so dispensable) simply to cast suspicion over the empress. But Gaozong was ready to believe Wu. He dismissed his wife, and made Wu Zhao his official consort. Not taking any chances, Wu had Wang Yu and another leading concubine, Xiao, arrested. On her orders, they were beaten and had their hands and feet cut off. They were then tossed into a cask of wine and left to die.

Opposite: Yang Guifei leaves her bath (18th century).

As the years went by and Gaozong's health began to worsen, Wu took an ever more assertive role at court. Soon, it's said, the emperor was beginning to wonder whether he had been wise in giving her so much power. No matter, she saw off all threats to her authority so successfully that, as Dowager Empress from 683, she remained unshiftable, and in 690 she made herself China's first and only female emperor. She was deposed in a coup by courtiers in 705, and died a few months later.

Below: The ultimate femme fatale, Wu Zhao wrapped Gaozong around her little finger – and, as his widow, reigned as China's empress.

AN LUSHAN'S ANARCHY

The Tang era was one of prosperity and progress in China, with great achievements in everything from astronomy to poetry, from philosophy to science. It was also a time of great stability and social order – until, that is, the empire was ripped apart by An Lushan's rebellion in 755. An Lushan (c. 703–57) was of uncertain origin. Although believed to have been of Central Asian Turkic descent, he had carved out a successful career as a soldier for the Chinese and risen to great eminence and wealth under the protection of Emperor Xuanzong.

An Lushan's army's capture of Luoyang sent a shockwave through the Chinese state that was only redoubled when he

BEAUTIFUL BUT DANGEROUS

The 'Four Beauties' of Chinese history loom larger in the folk memory than in any of the written sources. Still, the national narrative is much embellished by their presence. Of Xi Shi (who lived some time during the seventh century BCE), it was said that, when they beheld her face reflected in the river water as she leaned over – a dutiful worker – to wash her yarn, the awestruck fishes forgot how to swim and sank. When they looked down to see Wang Zhaojun, the flower of the first century BCE's Western Han Dynasty, the very geese fell out of the sky in sheer wonder. Diaochan, in the Three Kingdoms period was so ravishingly beautiful that the moon hid her face behind a cloud in shame.

Yang Guifei (719–56) comes closest of the four to having had a real, substantial and historically attested existence. She was a concubine, and subsequently consort, to Emperor Xuanzong (685–762). She had been married to one of the emperor's youngest sons when she first met him, but he was immediately smitten. Soon she was his inseparable companion, to whom nothing would be denied. Some 700 tailors and seamstresses toiled full-time keeping her wardrobe fresh.

Being 'high-maintenance' may have fallen within the job description of an imperial consort, but Yang Guifei flew high politically as well. She started doing favours, fixing positions and pensions, for her relatives. Xuanzong's choice of chancellor, Yang Guozhong, was a second cousin of hers who would never have come near the imperial court without her recommendation. She became closer than was wise with the arrogant and wayward general An Lushan – although in this she took her cue from her husband, who for years had spoiled this son-figure with favour and praise.

Such was Yang Guifei's beauty and charisma, though, that she was disruptive despite herself. Admiring courtiers competed for her attentions. It had been his jealousy of her attentions to Yang Guozhong, it was suggested, that had spurred An Lushan into his desperate rebellion. He had been so afraid of being marginalized that he had lashed out. Although the facts remain obscure, it seems that the consort ended up an accessory of some sort to An Lushan's actions. Reluctantly, the emperor agreed to have her strangled for her part in this betrayal – although he would never cease mourning his lost love.

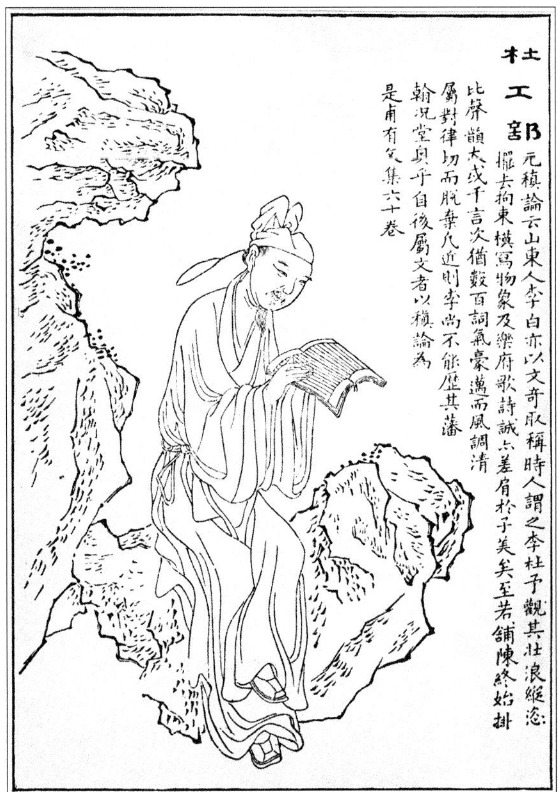

Above: Seen here in characteristically contemplative mood, the poet Du Fu was impassioned in his laments over the devastation brought about by An Lushan's Rebellion.

proclaimed himself emperor, and the founder of a new Yan Dynasty. As he marched against the empire's western capital, Chang'an, his sometime patron Xuanzong was forced to flee. He was not to lose his empire, though. An Lushan's bid to break out of his stronghold in the north of the country was ultimately unsuccessful, even if it took seven years (and two subsequent imperial reigns) for his rebellion to be put down.

Although the rebellion continued, An Lushan himself had been murdered by his own henchmen just a couple of years in, by which time it was already evident that 'Yan China' was not going to happen. Even so, the unrest once started seemed to have acquired its own momentum. When it finally finished, the fighting had claimed anything up to 36 million lives – a death toll unequalled until the days of World War II.

By the time an approximation of peace returned in 763, centralized government and civic order were a distant memory. Agricultural production was sporadic at best. 'Do you know,' asked the famous Mandarin poet Du Fu (712–77) rhetorically:

that, in two hundred districts east of the mountains,
In thousands of villages, weeds are the only harvest grown,
And while the women have worked hard to plough the earth,
Its furrows have been broken, east and west?

RURAL RESISTANCE

Slowly, over time, the Tang Dynasty recovered its poise and rebuilt the structures of the state, but it was never to be as confident as it had been before. Although the emperors' reign seemed secure at the centre, out in the empire low-level unrest was becoming normal. Peasant uprisings flared against a background of brigandage.

In practice, it was not always easy to distinguish between pure agrarian unrest and banditry. Desperate men and women, from marginalized communities, felt their only recourse was to turn to crime. Nor did it strike them that, in robbing wealthy travellers on local roads, they were attacking any social fabric they could recognize.

In any case, the two came together in 874, when Wang Xianzhi led his rebellion in Xinxiang, Henan province. Peasants stretched to the limit by a series of devastating floods believed they were not getting the support they needed from central government. They eagerly responded to Wang Xianzhi's call to arms. As his 'army' cut a swathe across the countryside of Henan and Shandong, it attracted new recruits in the tens of thousands. Emperor Xizong (862–88) sent troops to put down the insurgency, but it had acquired unstoppable momentum.

Not until 878 was Wang Xianzhi's force defeated. He himself was killed on the battlefield at Huangmei (near Huanggang in

Below: A map charts the progress of Wang Xianzhi's and Huang Chao's uprisings. Much of China was thrown into tumult by their revolts.

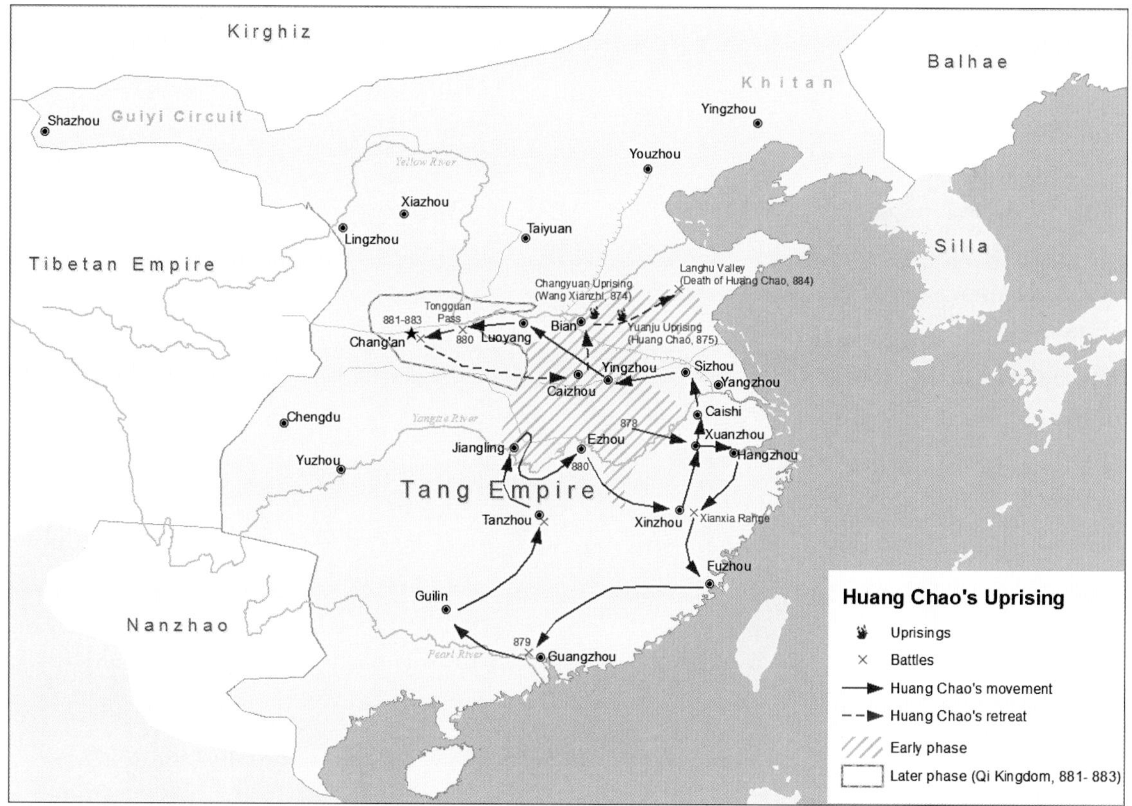

Hubei province). Even then, a section of his force got away. Under the leadership of Huang Chao (835–84), who until now had made his career as a salt smuggler, it carried on with Wang Xianzhi's fight. Under his leadership, the insurrection – already brutal – took on a particularly ugly nationalistic tone. His force is said to have massacred up to 200,000 foreign merchants and seafarers in the southern port of Guangzhou (Guangdong province).

Huang headed north again, occupying territories and seizing cities seemingly at will. In 881, he inflicted the ultimate humiliation on Emperor Xizong, forcing him to flee Chang'an. Having installed himself in the Tang capital, he proclaimed himself emperor in

FOOT BINDING

IT SEEMS TO HAVE been in this era that the practice of foot binding became fashionable for Chinese women, beginning with the courtly elite, but trickling down over time to all but the peasantry.

The custom started, by tradition, at the court of the kingdom of Southern Tang. One of the 'Ten Kingdoms', Southern Tang seems to have had only the most tenuous connection with the actual Tang Dynasty (now defunct), but its kings still claimed imperial lineage. It was at the request of one of these, the 'Emperor' Li Yu (c. 937–78), that Yao Niang, a concubine, first bound her feet. Tradition has it that she tied them tightly with white silk bands so that they would resemble crescent moons as she danced atop a jewel- and pearl-encrusted golden lotus. Another story says that a fox-spirit came up with the idea when she took the form of a princess to seduce a powerful king: this was a cunning way of concealing her tell-tale paws. These are entertaining stories, but the reality of foot binding was excruciating. Women in many different times and cultures have suffered to maintain socially imposed ideals of beauty, teetering along on impractically high heels or having their abdominal organs crushed by corsets. It is hard, however, to think of any fashion that has been more cruel than that of foot binding, as carried out in China for many centuries.

Starting around the age of five, while the bones were still comparatively soft and malleable and the foot still 'naturally'

Xizong's place. He was not to enjoy the privileges of this pretended office for long, however. In 883, he was dislodged from Chang'an and forced on to the defensive. The following year, a Tang army caught up with him in Yanzhou, Shandong, and inflicted a disastrous defeat. Huang is said to have been betrayed at the last by his own nephew, who turned himself in to the authorities, bringing his late uncle's head with him as a peace offering.

Betrayal became the fashion, but it went both ways. Zhu Wen (852–912), a former comrade of Huang's who went over to the government side, became so powerful that, in 907, he toppled the Tang Dynasty to reign as Emperor Taizu.

Below: Footbinding produced hideous disfigurements in the name of beauty. But the fashion held sway for centuries in China.

small, it was bound up tightly with bandage-like strips to hinder growth. While the big toe was left in its old position, the others were tucked up underneath against the sole to make a narrow point. Meanwhile, the arch of the foot was (quite literally and physically) broken so the heel and ball of the foot could be compressed together and the whole foot crushed up into a 'lotus' shape just a few inches long.

Agonizing as the initial binding process was, there was to be no appreciable relief thereafter, as the bandages had to be kept permanently in place. Indeed, they had to be endlessly renewed as the girl grew older and her feet kept doing their best to grow.

Hygiene, as well as fashionable aesthetics, demanded that the bindings be removed for the foot to be cleaned, its nails trimmed and infections treated. While the bandages were off, the bones and muscles would be pummelled to ensure soft pliability before fresh bindings were applied and pulled to the utmost tightness.

High fashion in every culture has almost invariably been impractical. That has been partly the point: to confer prestige by advertising the wearer's freedom from the need to attend to the normal duties of domestic or other work. Foot binding went further, though, rendering the Chinese woman barely able to walk – her teetering, swaying steps are said to have been part of her allure. It has been suggested that the wasted hips and thighs that resulted from this cruel crippling may have helped to eroticize her appearance further.

The Tang Dynasty had been trapped. The more it had militarized in response to insubordination across the empire, the more powerful it had made warrior strongmen in the regions. The armies that had assured its integrity had at the same time guaranteed its fall. The name historians have given to the period that followed – that of the 'Five Dynasties and Ten Kingdoms' – is not so much a description as an exclamation of despair. Through the first half of the 10th century, small states were to rise and fall with mesmerizing speed as military leaders vied with one another for advantage.

The dynasties of the period's name ruled successively in the northern territories; the 'kingdoms' lay – mostly simultaneously, but with a dizzying succession of different rulers – across the south. Despite this anarchy, China as a cultural project continued to progress. Great art and literature were produced during this time.

Below: Taizu of Song may have seized power by force and held on to it tyrannically, but he did succeed in making China strong.

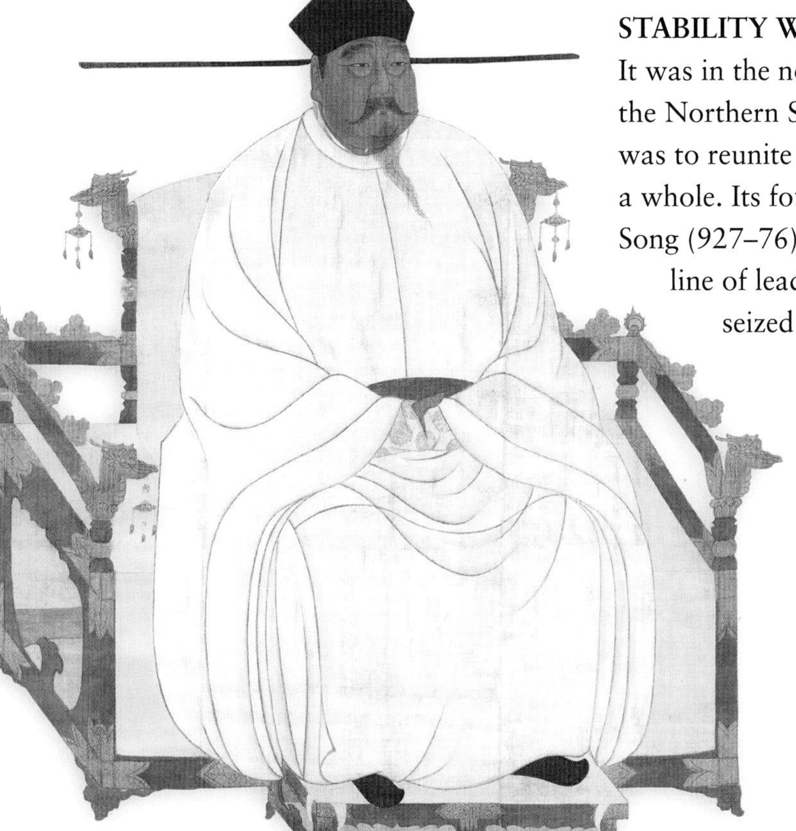

STABILITY WITH THE SONG

It was in the north that a sixth dynasty, the Northern Song, at last emerged that was to reunite the realms of China as a whole. Its founder, Emperor Taizu of Song (927–76), was the latest in a long line of leading generals who had seized imperial power for himself. He differed from his predecessors, however, first in making himself secure in his northern heartland and second in making significant conquests among the kingdoms of the south. These gains were consolidated from 976 by his younger brother and successor, Taizong (939–97).

It was whispered that Emperor Taizu's death might not have been accidental. Contemporaries claimed that he had been murdered by Taizong. These suspicions were not allayed by the death just three years later of Taizu's son, Prince Zhao Dezhao (951–79). He was said to have committed suicide – although some at court were sceptical.

However ill gotten his throne, Taizong turned out to be a credit to it. He was certainly true to his late brother's imperial mission in bringing stability to the realm, not only by making conquests and recreating the old imperial China but also by rebuilding and reinforcing its institutions. Under the Song, the civil service was restored to its former glory.

There was nothing boring about 'bureaucracy' in 10th-century China. A beefed-up officialdom, Taizu and Taizong both seem to have appreciated, was the empire's best defence against government by a succession of opportunistic military thugs. That the promotion of this clerical class helped foster an outpouring of cultural creativity was of secondary importance to the Song.

IT WAS WHISPERED THAT EMPEROR TAIZU'S DEATH MIGHT NOT HAVE BEEN ACCIDENTAL.

RAIDERS FROM THE NORTH

As so many times before in Chinese history, these developments in civilization were overshadowed by the threat from the north. There had never been any shortage of nomad raiders from the Asian steppe.

A succession of peoples, emerging here, had attacked the empire's northern and western frontiers and, in many cases, settled in frontier regions for the longer term. After the Khitan, from Mongolia, had come the Tanguts (from up against what is now the Tibetan border). In the 12th century, it was the turn of the Jurchen, from Manchuria. They built their Jin Empire across an extensive tranche of northern China.

The Song Dynasty was forced to transfer its capital from northerly Kaifeng to Li'nan (Hangzhou). The armies of this Southern Song succeeded in holding back the Jurchen, and so an uneasy equilibrium was maintained.

GENGHIS KHAN

THE MONGOLS WERE JUST one of many nomadic pastoralist peoples who had sprung up over the centuries in the vastness of the steppe, but they were to make their mark on world history in a way none of their predecessors had, building the largest land empire ever seen.

The man who made them a conquering nation is universally known as 'Genghis Khan', but this was a title, not his name. Translating, roughly, as 'Mightiest King', it was earned in blood and toil by one 'Temujin' (c. 1165–1227). His father, Yesugei, had been a minor chieftain, and had died when Temujin was young. Without his father's protection, the boy had been ostracized and forced to learn how to stand up for himself.

Temujin gathered a group of young fighters around him with sheer courage and charisma; they stayed with him on account of his effectiveness in war.

By 1206, he had won his title as Khagan – Khan or leader of all the Mongols – forging a united people out of an ill-sorted array of squabbling tribes. He had also created a spectacularly successful war machine, as the peoples of China, India, the Middle East and Europe were to find out.

THE MONGOLS ON THE MOVE

Above: Kublai Khan may have enthusiastically adopted the civilized virtues of his Chinese subjects, but he had his share of ruthlessness as well.

Opposite: Genghis Khan is here commemorated by an appropriately-outsized statue, standing 40m (130ft) tall, atop a 10m (33ft) plinth.

In 1207, the Mongols exploded out of the vastness of the steppe under the leadership of the terrifying Genghis Khan. In the years that followed, he led his forces deep into northern China, before sweeping westward across the steppes of Central Asia. Northern India, southern Russia, Afghanistan, Iran and the eastern Arab empire all faced the ferocity of the Mongols. Genghis Khan died in 1227, but his sons continued where he had left off: soon the Mongol empire stretched all the way from the Pacific to the plains of Eastern Europe.

In 1260, this enormous realm was split in two: the eastern part, including present-day Mongolia, fell to Genghis Khan's grandson, Kublai Khan (1215–94). It was clear that he saw China as something more than a source of plunder. Indeed, he appears to have done his best to become Chinese himself. Establishing his capital at Khanbalik (now Beijing), he renounced his claims on all other Mongol territories, devoting his energies entirely to the rule of China.

It would be wrong to see Kublai Khan as a sinophile in any simple, sentimental way: he had been campaigning against the Southern Song when the news of his succession reached him in 1259. Nor, despite his evident love of civilization, could he be characterized as a man of peace. Although nominally Khagan from the following year, he faced a bitter succession struggle with his younger brother, Ariq Böke (c. 1219–66). It was not till 1264 that he was able to return to his long-term plans.

Kublai Khan was, however, a keen admirer of all things Chinese – especially of Chinese technology and wealth. And if he couldn't wait to add the 'Middle Kingdom' to the Mongol Empire, he showed real respect for his imperial possession.

Taking the title of Huangdi or 'Emperor' in 1279, he gave a Chinese name, Yuan ('first'), to the dynasty he was founding. The title was an empty one, in that he didn't yet have any meaningful control over most of the territories he was claiming. Even so, it would have meant something to his Chinese subjects. Kublai Khan was signalling that he came not just as a conqueror but as a kindred spirit. He underlined this by establishing his capital on Chinese soil, in Daidu, or Beijing. How deep his self-reinvention as a Chinese ruler really ran is hard to know: he went to some trouble in his reform programme to recast Chinese society along Mongol lines.

XIANGYANG UNDER SIEGE

Kublai Khan was not shy about waging war with his adoptive country. He began by laying siege to the city of Xiangyang. This centre was strategically vital, since it controlled access to

Below: It took six years, but Kublai Khan was finally to take Xiangyang. The arrows show where he made his final assault.

the Han River and hence to the Yangtze, and from there to the fertile and populous plains of central China. Kublai Khan attacked with 100,000 mounted warriors.

Expecting a siege, he had come equipped with trebuchets – catapults that could fling heavy rocks across the river into the city. At least, they would have been able to, had not the Song defenders, in readiness, widened the river at the crucial point and padded their walls with netting. This ensured that the missiles that hit them were rendered harmless. Kublai Khan, contemporary sources say, responded by building a fleet of 5000 ships to blockade the river. But the Song had stocked up well with provisions and were able to hold out almost indefinitely – especially when, after many failed attempts, a relief force managed to break through with fresh supplies.

In the end, they held out for six years. If this was testimony to their courage and resolution, it was a tribute too to the temperament of a nomad leader, who might not have been expected to show such patience. The breakthrough, when it came, was brought about in large part by the introduction of new, counterweighted trebuchets that could send 300kg (660lb) missiles a distance of 500m (1640ft). Kublai Khan had brought the Muslim military engineers Ismail and Ala al-Din all the way from Persia (or perhaps Iraq) specifically to design and build these weapons for him.

Left: Mongol trebuchets were extremely advanced for their time.

Xiangyang had been the Song's strongest fortress: once it was taken, there was nothing to stop the Mongols from streaming west and south through the heart of China. By 1276, most of the country was in Mongol hands.

The Song's last stand came in March 1279. The Battle of Yamen, a naval engagement, came as the conclusion of another siege – this time at sea. Although far outnumbered, the Yuan ships had succeeded in confining the Song fleet in a narrow bay. They had kept up a blockade to cut off supplies of food and water. The Song commander had his hundreds of ships lashed together in a line to prevent any flight or breaking of formation, but this also effectively stopped them from manoeuvring. When the Mongols attacked, moreover, their warriors were afforded a floating walkway across which they could reach the Song flagship in the centre.

Above: Sophisticated siege defences made the challenge for attackers that much tougher.

Kublai Khan's achievement in conquering China had been extraordinary. The celebrated victories were really just the start. He had contrived a minor miracle of organization and logistical support and sustained it over the best part of a decade and over several thousand kilometres in a country that could hardly have been less well suited to the traditional tactics of the Mongols.

The question of his state's 'Chinese'-ness takes on a new importance at this point in the narrative. Do the imperialist adventures he now embarked upon belong to the history of the Mongols or of China? One attempt at a seaborne invasion of Japan had been beaten back by what the Japanese would come to call a *kamikaze* ('divine wind') in 1274. A second fleet was sent in 1281. This one, like its predecessor, landed troops at Hakata Bay, Kyushu. Again, a blessed storm came and scattered the invaders' ships. In hindsight, these look less like acts of god than lapses in preparation by an inexperienced and naive commander. Kublai Khan's ships seem to have been quickly and carelessly built; many were not much more than riverboats.

An invasion of Burma in 1277 exposed further limitations in the Mongol war machine. Kublai Khan's forces conquered the country easily, but could not hold it, and for the most banal of reasons: the difficult part of the conquest achieved, they found themselves beaten back by heat. They were frustrated too in repeated invasions of Vietnam (1284–5 and 1287–8). The Vietnamese, who gave up their towns without serious resistance, then mounted a dogged guerrilla campaign in the countryside, would find inspiration in this episode when they faced the Americans 700 years later.

That sort of resistance might have posed serious problems in Koguryo, Korea, nominally a possession since 1260. Here, however, Kublai Khan employed more guile. Rather than mounting full-scale invasions, he provided discreet support to King Wonjong (1219–74) against his rivals: in return, he won Korea's loyalty as a vassal state.

Below: A storm smashes Kublai Khan's invasion fleet, in passage for Japan.

OVERWHELMED

When Kublai Khan died in 1294, he was followed by his grandson Temur (1265–1307) – but his succession was as troublesome as Kublai Khan's had been. Later Yuan emperors lacked the intelligence, the integrity or the administrative skills to reign successfully over such an enormous empire. Beset by

MARCO'S MYTHS?

THE VENETIAN TRAVELLER MARCO Polo (1254–1324) opened up the Orient to Europe. That is how he has conventionally been seen, at least. As the preface to his own memoir makes clear, his father and his uncle had made an earlier visit to China in 1260. They had been asked by Kublai Khan to return with 100 missionaries to teach his people about Christianity and Western culture. By the time they set out on this second trip in 1271, Marco was 17 years old, so old enough to accompany them on a journey that was to take them away from Venice for almost a quarter of a century.

Marco, we are told, saw many wonders on his journey to the East. On arriving in China, the Italians were warmly welcomed by the emperor. Charmed by his young visitor, he made Marco an official agent, sending him off to carry messages to, and bring back reports on, every corner of the empire.

The memoir we know as *The Travels of Marco Polo* (c. 1300) was co-written with Rustichello da Pisa, a well-known writer of romances – who actually named the narrative *The Book of the Marvels of the World*. On the one hand, it includes encounters with cannibal tribes and other exotica; on the other, it features convincing descriptions of important cities, such as Hangzhou and Jining. So although it makes sense to take the *Travels* with a pinch of salt, it is also important to be aware that many of its less extravagant details are corroborated by Arab, Persian and other Eastern writers of the time.

Some more sceptical scholars suggest that these Asian authorities did not so much endorse Polo's testimony as account for it – by providing the sources that he then plagiarized. Historian Frances Wood has pointed out that there is no definitive proof of Polo having ventured beyond the Black Sea on his journey to the East, and any amount of evidence that he did not actually go to China. He does not, she points out, use Chinese place names – surprising in one who is supposed to have travelled so widely and over so many years on the emperor's behalf. Neither does he appear to have noticed such striking features as the Great Wall, nor the phenomenon of foot binding,

chronic problems of overstretch, they attempted to fund soaring military expenditure by ramping up the taxes on the rural poor.

A series of droughts in the 1330s alternated with a succession of floods that prompted the Yellow River to change course and spill across several cities. In the process, it rendered the Grand Canal unusable, crippling commerce across much of central

Below: The Polos present a letter from Pope Clement IV to a (distinctly Caucasian-looking) Kublai Khan. An illumination from a medieval manuscript.

among many other Chinese customs.

But if Polo was unobservant, Wood points out, Chinese officials were still worse. No one, she notes, in the whole vast and elaborate hierarchy of the imperial civil service, thought at any point to record the presence of so exotic and so seemingly important an assistant to the emperor.

and eastern China. The resort to coastal sea routes fostered an upsurge in piracy. In 1344, the Yuan emperor Toqto'a (1314–56) came up with an ambitious scheme to canalize the Yellow River's lower reaches. Under the plan, the river would be returned to its ancient course. That meant diverting it so it would reach the sea to the south of the Shandong Peninsula rather than (as had been the case for the last few centuries) the north.

This was a visionary – and eminently successful – project. Again, however, it was one whose burden was to fall not upon the emperor but on his people. More than 170,000 of them were called up as corvéed labour. The remainder faced further taxation on top of the just about unbearable burden they were already carrying. Popular resentment found a racial focus in the Red Turban Rebellion. This broke out in 1351, pitching the Chinese against the Mongols – once more regarded as an occupying force.

Like the Yellow Turban Rebellion 1200 years before, this movement took its name from the colour its adherents wore; it too had originated in a religious sect (a Buddhist one this time, the

Below: The Emperor Temur takes time out from a troubled, turbulent reign, hunting with his courtiers in the countryside.

White Lotus group), but had acquired a more secular, nationalist energy as it spread. Zhu Yuanzhang (1328–98) emerged as its leader. Hampered by continuing environmental and economic problems, the Yuan Dynasty felt increasingly beleaguered.

TYRANNY AND TORTURE

The Yuan Dynasty was finally toppled in 1368. Zhu Yuanzhang seized power and made himself the first Ming Emperor of China, reigning as Hongwu. His rule was to be tyrannical, but, he seems to have reasoned, it was at least Chinese. He could not really

Left: A young Zhu Yuanzhang begins his novitiate as a Buddhist monk. There's no hint here of the violence his future was to hold.

BLACK DEATH

THE LIST OF CHINESE 'firsts' is famously a long and impressive one, encompassing everything from acupuncture to iron smelting. Understandably less lauded is the country's role in unleashing the plague on an unsuspecting world. Most famous in the 'bubonic' form, which creates painful swellings or 'buboes' in the armpits and groin, the plague was responsible for the 'Black Death' that is believed to have killed some 60 per cent of the population of Western Europe around 1346–50.

It was, however, an immigrant in China too. *Yersinia pestis*, the bacterium responsible for plague, is known to have been endemic in Central Asia. Left to itself, it existed more or less harmlessly in the fleas infesting the fur of marmots and other ground rodents. These animals stayed well away from human settlements, living far out in the empty steppe.

Researchers in recent years have discovered that the earliest traces of the mutation that caused the plague in humans emerged in China some time around 600 BCE. Notoriously, it was carried by *Rattus rattus*, the black rat, which liked to live in close proximity with humans. It was in China too that, in 1331–4, 'Outbreak Zero' of the Black Death is believed to have taken place. By 1353, two-thirds of the population had perished, according to the chroniclers. In Hebei province alone, officials estimated, more than five million people had fallen victim to the plague – 90 per cent of the population of that time.

Western Europe has not seen a significant outbreak of the plague since the 17th century. Through much of the developed world, indeed, the threat is seen as inherently historical. So it has been in China too, for the most part. As recently as 2014, however, a case was reported in the city of Yumen, in northwest China's Gansu province. More than 150 people had to be quarantined and the city as a whole temporarily sealed off.

have been called a nationalist – the idea of the nation as we know it did not yet exist – but he defined himself and his authority against that of the Yuan Dynasty, a regime of foreigners, imposed on China by invasive force.

Above: Hongwu cut a thuggish figure. He was viewed with a fear that was justifiable given his readiness to have his critics killed and tortured.

An uneducated man of peasant origins, who for a time in his youth had literally lived as a beggar, the new emperor feared and distrusted the old clerical elite. Hongwu's persecution of the scholarly establishment made Shihuangdi's seem mild: many thousands were exiled; many were put to death. Not only did he execute the first minister he believed was contemplating toppling him, along with hundreds of his staff, but also he abolished his position – and made it a capital offence to even suggest its reinstatement.

Torture was central to Hongwu's system. He was an enthusiast for the punishment of the slow and painful death. He shared Shihuangdi's feeling that it was more important to be feared than admired or loved. Unsurprisingly, few officials even thought of voicing criticisms. One courageous man who did, and who was summoned to see Hongwu, it's said, took his own coffin with him. Once he had finished delivering his report, he climbed in to await his inevitable death. The emperor was apparently so amused in his sadistic way that he relented and spared the official's life.

Hongwu's tyranny was even-handed in the sense that, however cruel and capricious he was in his dealings with the empire's elites, he was every bit as oppressive to the common people. Rebels, or even suspected rebels, were summarily flayed as an example to others. Noticeboards in every village bore the emperor's 'Great Warnings' of the consequences of disobedience and disorder.

Opposite: Relief workers attend to a 1911 outbreak of plague.

Like other dictators, Hongwu got things done. It helped that he felt no empathy for the thousands of families he uprooted as he set about remodelling his realms. Whole populations were moved to resettle war- and famine-ravaged northern areas. Noble families were brought to his new capital at Nanjing. He sent imperial princes (and potential usurpers) to occupy military positions on his frontiers.

BATTLE OF LAKE POYANG

The biggest, bloodiest naval engagement in history seems to have been fought, not on any sea or ocean, but in the fresh waters of a Chinese lake in 1363. Laying siege to the rebel stronghold of Nanchang, in Jiangxi province, the Yuan commander Chen Youliang (1320–63) saw that cutting off access to the city from the landward side would be pointless if supplies and reinforcements could still be shipped in across the adjacent lake. Accordingly, he brought up more than 100 vessels to blockade a city already surrounded on the landward side.

Big, well equipped and full to the gunnels with soldiers, his fleet included a considerable number of tall, formidably armoured 'tower ships' (*see illustration*). From these wall-dwarfing vessels he hoped to launch his final assault upon the stubborn city. Unfortunately for him, it did not turn out that way.

Instead, a resourceful Zhu Yuanzhang approached undaunted with his much smaller fleet. Setting several vessels on fire, he steered them towards the tower ships. In the end, he secured an improbable victory – although one that bore a resemblance to Liu Bei's and Sun Quan's at the Battle of Red Cliffs and that, although historical, has become an important Chinese myth. More than half a million Yuan soldiers and sailors are said to have died.

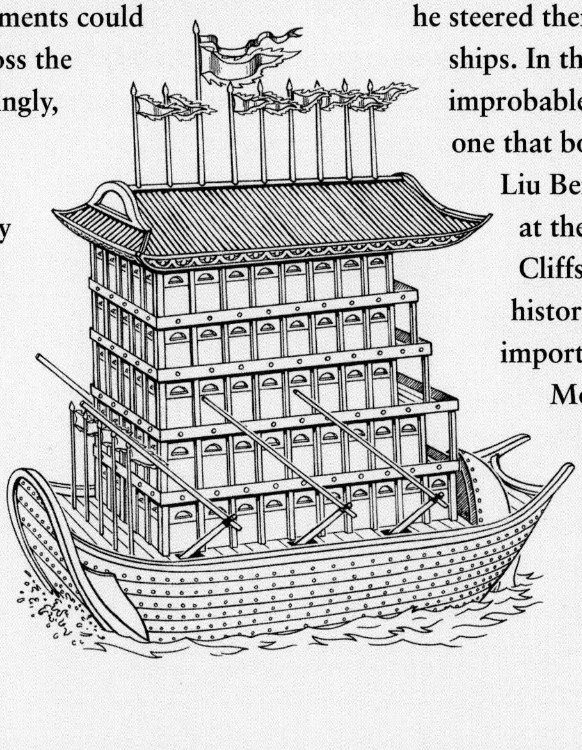

Despite his actions, Hongwu could not feel secure. The Mongols, although down, were not yet out. The army of 150,000 men that Hongwu sent to Mongolia to exact tribute in 1372 was all but eliminated in an epic battle on the banks of the Tuul River.

This was a reminder that the security of Hongwu's Ming Dynasty could not be complacently relied upon. He reorganized and enlarged his imperial army and built the world's largest naval dockyard at Nanjing. But he deployed his military forces as freely at home (against real or imaginary opposition) as he did abroad. His favourite general, Chang Yuchun (1330–69), was accused of committing multiple atrocities as he put down rebellions in Shandong and Hunan.

Below: Chang Yuchun was a general of great flair but, in his loyalty to Hongwu, he would commit barbaric crimes against civilians.

POWER AND PARANOIA

Hongwu's wariness towards his relatives does not appear to have been misplaced. He himself appears to have died a natural death at the respectable age of 70. Even so, his doctors were executed along with his concubines, on his own orders. But his grandson and successor, the Jianwen Emperor (1377–1402), was to be bullied by his uncles – and, after what amounted to a civil war, was overthrown and killed by one of them, Zhu Di (1360–1424), the Yongle Emperor.

Despite its ugly start, Yongle's reign was a success, although it had its unappealing aspects, especially for its Confucian scholars. Like Shihuangdi and Hongwu, Yongle had a deep distrust for intellectuals, and for their grasp of recent history in particular. He hoped that, by suppressing such learning, he could suppress the memory of his rise to power, disreputable and violent as that had been.

Opposite: Despite his own personal paranoia, the Yongle Emperor ensured that China opened up commercially and diplomatically to the outside world.

It seems to have been the same sort of paranoia that prompted Yongle's move in 1403 to a new northern capital at Beiping (Beijing), where he would have a blank slate to start his reign, and his construction there of a 'Forbidden City', within whose walls he could retreat. The part that had previously been played by scholars in the administration of the empire was increasingly taken up by a corps of eunuchs, whose loyalties lay with the emperor rather than the wider state.

TOURS DE FORCE

Under Yongle's direction, Ming China was looking outward, both in military strategy and trade. No one did more to promote this policy than the emperor's trusted eunuch, Zheng He (1371–1433). A Muslim by upbringing, he had been castrated in adulthood after his capture by the Chinese as a prisoner-of-war. He had gone on to become a personal attendant to Zhu Di, whom he had helped seize power in 1402.

THE TREASURE FLEET'S TOURS WERE DIFFERENT FROM THE COLONIALISM OF THE EUROPEAN POWERS.

Now, with his master's backing, Zheng He found a new vocation as an admiral, leading a succession of voyages by the emperor's so-called 'Treasure Fleet'. The first expedition, which embarked in 1405, sailed south via Vietnam to Indonesia before pushing west to Ceylon (Sri Lanka) and India. Subsequent expeditions took the Treasure Fleet as far as the Persian Gulf, Arabia and East Africa. The suggestion that Zheng He circumnavigated the globe and 'discovered' America is not supported by any serious evidence. Camels, leopards, rhinoceroses, giraffes and ostriches were just a few of the exotic animals brought back to China from these travels. The explorations went on throughout Yongle's reign and into those of his son and short-lived successor, the Hongxi Emperor (1378–1425) and his son, the Xuande Emperor (1399–1435).

The Treasure Fleet's tours were different in kind from the colonialism of the European powers. Although its giant vessels were impressively well armed, and so its presentation intimidating, this seems to have been overwhelmingly for show. The Battle of Palembang apart (when, in 1407, the Chinese took on a fleet of pirates off the Sumatran port and killed 5000), there is no record

of any significant military action being undertaken. Nor were any territories occupied or bases established: the Chinese Empire already had as much land and resources as it knew what to do with. These forays by its Treasure Fleet were more about what we might now call the projection of soft power. Diplomatic and commercial relations were forged with the countries visited.

Below: China had always arguably been the pre-eminent power in eastern Asia. Under Yongle it asserted its authority across the region.

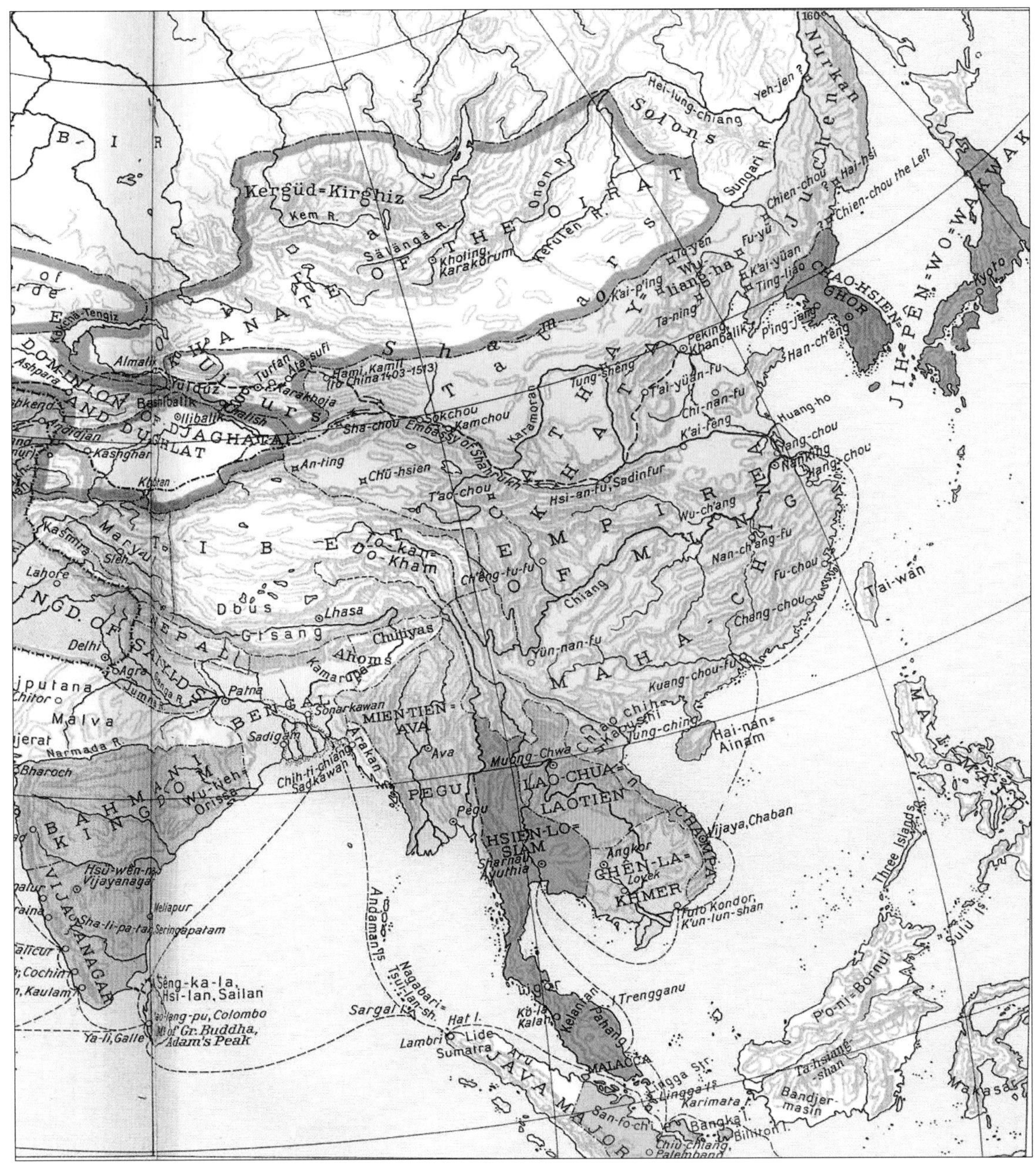

DISPUTED DISPLACEMENTS

MODERN MARINE ENGINEERS ARE sceptical about contemporary claims that the Ming treasure ships could be up to 120m (400ft) long – it is hard to see how wood-built structures of such dimensions could conceivably have held together out at sea. Testimony abounds, however, from both Eastern and Western witnesses, that the Chinese were building gigantic four- or five-masted ocean-going junks. Inscriptions from temples of the time suggest that ships of 500 tons were routinely being put to sea. The Italian merchant Niccolò de' Conti (c. 1395–1469), who spent some years in Southeast Asia, claimed to have seen Chinese vessels four times that size.

There would have been considerable variation in the size of ships sent out. The Treasure Ships themselves were attended by a range of smaller vessels, specially designed to defend the fleet in case of attack or to carry everything from horses to supplies of water.

There is dispute too over the number of ships involved in the expeditions of the Chinese Treasure Fleet. One source says that Zheng He's first expedition was undertaken by 317 ships in total; another estimates the figure as 250; a third a more modest 62. Even this last account, however, suggests a total number of crew approaching 28,000 – an average of well over 400 men per ship.

Historical estimates for subsequent expeditions more or less agree on numbers: fleets of 200-odd ships were crewed by totals of around 20,000 men. This consensus could mean that the approximations are correct. Conversely, it might just mean that they are equally incorrect – all being drawn from the same, essentially unreliable, original source.

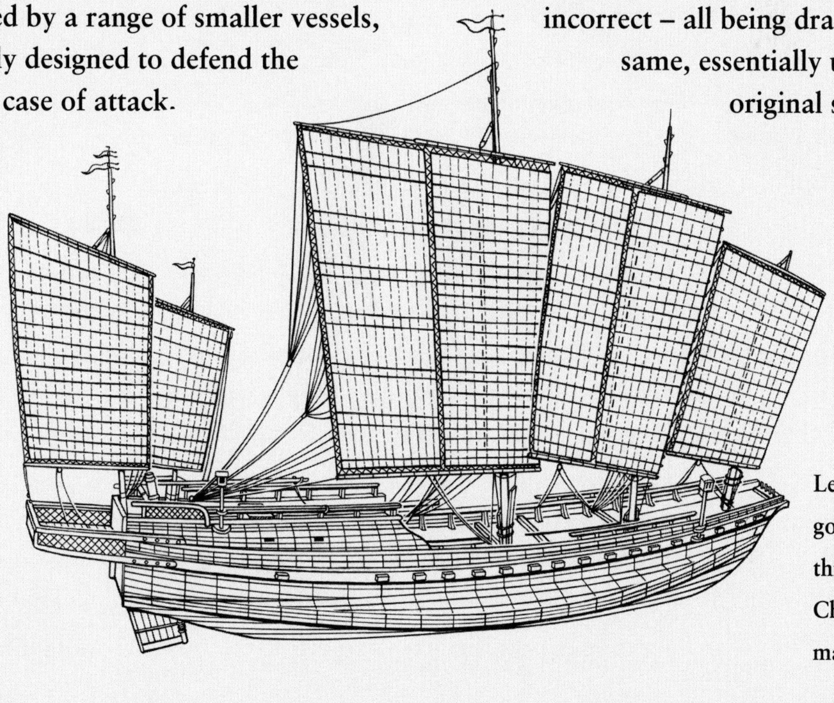

Left: Big, ocean-going junks like this one made Ming China a major maritime power.

These voyages of discovery and display were not 'dark' in themselves, but there was 'darkness' in the way the whole programme was shelved in the 1430s. The reason for this is not clear. It seems to have been in part a matter of palace politics, with the traditional nobility turning against an enterprise that was associated with the eunuch elite. It also seems to have reflected a general mood of mercantile and geopolitical introversion. If it did not reflect such a mood, it fairly quickly created one.

As the cultural climate in China changed, so did prevailing attitudes towards the outside world. The official perspective on the Treasure Fleet is illustrative of this. The enterprise had not only been discreetly dropped, it was also played down in the historical record. Works like *The History of Ming* (1739) may scrupulously mention the voyages of the Treasure Fleet – but 'mention' them is just about all they do. We get no sense from these early modern accounts of the epic ambition, the excitement and the glory of an exploratory adventure that pre-empted Europe's Age of Discovery by a generation. Instead, we get the beginnings of that isolationism that, over the following century or so, was to lend some credence to the Western stereotyping of Chinese society as in some way static – even atrophied. China really had rejected the world at large, it seemed.

CHINA REALLY HAD REJECTED THE WORLD AT LARGE, IT SEEMED.

ROUGH TREATMENT

The Tumu Crisis of 1449 cannot have done much for China's confidence. It began with a battle at Tumu Fortress, northwest of Beijing. Not only did a Mongol cavalry force some 20,000 strong annihilate an imperial army more than twenty times that size, it also captured Emperor Yingzong (1427–64) and held him hostage for four years.

Meanwhile, in the 16th century, with the Western Age of Discovery getting under way in earnest, the Chinese found themselves being bullied by the Portuguese. In 1513, with conflicting feelings, the Zhengde Emperor (1505–21) had accepted their establishment of a trading post at Tamão (Tuen

Mun, in the Pearl River Delta near Hong Kong). But their attempts to meddle in the empire's affairs irritated him, and in 1521 he had his navy expel them from their base.

The Battle of Tamão was a triumph for China; it was a profound humiliation for Portugal and a blow to Western prestige more widely. It did not really change things, however. The Portuguese quickly regrouped and founded a new settlement a few miles along the coast at Macau, from which, in the decades that followed, they continued to press Chinese communities into trading with them. Not only that: finding that their new colonies in India needed plantation labour, they mounted slave raids into China.

Below: The Battle of Tamão: the triumph of China over the Portuguese is brought vividly to life in this museum diorama.

THE SHAANXI EARTHQUAKE

Above: Soldiers struggle to save survivors from a much later Shaanxi earthquake, 2008.

'NOTHING IN HISTORY HAD ever surpassed it,' the scholar Qin Keda recalled of his experiences in the Shaanxi earthquake (1556). Nor, experts believed, has it been surpassed in all the centuries since. There have been more powerful tremors (it is believed to have registered a respectable but by no means unusual eight in magnitude), but none so devastating or so deadly. More than 800,000 people are believed to have been killed.

The effects of the earthquake were much exacerbated by geological factors: its destructive centre, in the Wei River valley outside Huaxian, in Shaanxi province, lay in an area of soft and crumbly loess. Deep cracks appeared in the earth; whole communities, living in caves or homes hollowed out of hillsides, were instantly entombed. In Huaxian itself, not a single dwelling was left standing.

'I woke with a start,' Qin Keda said. 'From my bed, it sounded as though someone was throwing pots and pans around; the clatter of tiles in my room was like the galloping hooves of a thousand horses. At first I thought of flight, thinking it was a disaster brought by demons. Only after, when I saw the entire wall collapsing where, moments earlier, my head had rested, did I suddenly realize that this was an earthquake.'

Through the space where his bedroom wall had been, Qin Keda could see what should have been a silver moon, its grubby face besmirched by clouds of floating dust. In the next room, he found his family – all alive, thankfully. But they could hardly hear one another for the roaring crash that now erupted. 'In that moment,' the scholar said, 'ten thousand houses were demolished; my ears were assaulted by the confusing din; I could make out nothing through the cacophony of cries.'

Such inclination as Ming China might have had to look beyond its own shores was discouraged by the growing menace in its coastal waters of the *Wokou*. The Chinese word *wo* meant 'dwarf', or, with obvious pejorativeness, 'Japanese'; *kou* meant 'robber' or 'bandit' – so the *wok*ou were 'dwarf-pirates'. In fact, many of them were homegrown (as many as 70 per cent, by some contemporary estimates), which made the label doubly derogatory.

BESIEGED BY PIRATES

Many of the *Wokou* were not even pirates in any normal sense. They made their living by smuggling or sanctions-busting. The strict prohibitions that the authorities had placed on foreign trade had created shortages of luxuries that many Chinese consumers wanted to secure. Ming China's xenophobic restrictions had, in

Below: A Chinese expedition sets out to do battle with the pirates of Japan, from a scroll dating back to the later days of the Ming Dynasty.

Opposite: He never did occupy the emperor's throne, but Nurhaci still had an imperial destiny as founder of the Manchu Dynasty.

other words, brought about a boom in black-market commerce and associated lawlessness, which – in a vicious circle – only underlined their sense of being under siege.

Soon enough, Ming China was to be attacked literally. By the 1580s, the Manchu were on the rise. What had started as a rebellion slowly transformed itself, first into an invasion, then into almost three centuries of rule by the Qing Dynasty.

Nurhaci (1559–1626), who brought the quarrelsome tribes together to form a single Manchu force, never got to reign as emperor. It was his son, Hong Taji (1592–1643), who took over in 1622, and reigned as the first Qing Emperor. Even so, his title was to some extent an overweening one in that most of China was still to be conquered by the time he died. His son, the Shunzhi Emperor (1638–61), just five years old when he received the Mandate of Heaven in 1643, was the first Qing ruler actually to reign in China.

DROWNING IN MISFORTUNE

IN ITS FINAL DAYS, the Ming Dynasty found itself fighting desperately on two fronts, not only against the Manchu, but also against a rebel force led by Li Zicheng (1606–45). The hopelessness of the emperor's situation was underlined by events around the city of Kaifeng (Henan province).

Here, after a six-month rebel siege, the provincial governor hit on the solution of emulating the action of Ying Zheng's general Wang Ben in 225 BCE.

Deliberately breaching the retaining embankments along the Yellow River, he caused a flood that he hoped would inundate and drown the attacking army. Instead, he inundated his own city and drowned more than 300,000 civilians. The episode seems emblematic somehow, especially because it was to no avail.

By 1644, the situation was growing hopeless and, on 26 May, Li Zicheng's troops entered Beijing. It was to be they who, technically, brought down the Ming with the overthrow of the Chongzhen Emperor (1611–44), although they were swiftly ousted by the Manchu when they arrived.

4

A World of Worries

Prosperous and powerful, Qing China could take pride in its self-sufficiency. But it was becoming hard to keep the outside world at bay.

Condescension, even contempt, is embedded in the very word 'Chinaman'. If for generations it served as a simple descriptive, used freely and unabashedly in the English language, that is not because it wasn't always obviously derogatory but because being derogatory about non-European races was not deemed offensive. It can hardly come as a surprise, then, that a nation referred to with the verbal equivalent of racist caricature was literally caricatured in pictorial depictions.

QUESTIONS OF COIFFURE

After the eyes, and the conical 'coolie' hat, the most immediate marker for the cartoon Chinaman was his hair – shaved short above his brow, but bound into a long pigtail or 'queue' hanging down behind. It is tempting to dismiss the representation of this feature as just so much racist stereotyping – and for the most part that was its intent. However, it was also factual: for the

Opposite: A dominant force in imperial politics from the 1880s to the 1900s, the Dowager Empress Cixi wasn't quite forceful enough to arrest China's decline.

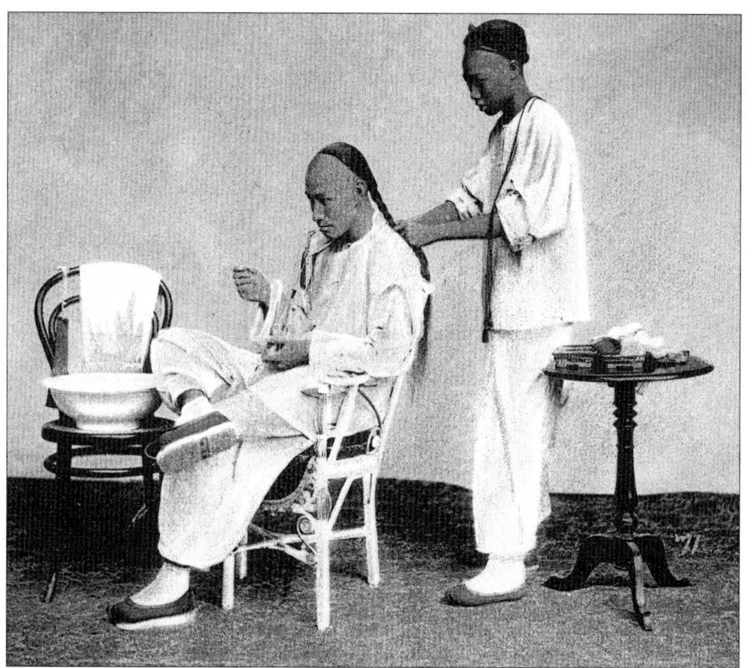

Above: The 'queue' became the internationally-acknowledged marker of the Chinese male. Not surprisingly: its wearing was enforced by Manchu law.

almost 300 years of the Qing Dynasty's reign, this hairstyle was imposed on Chinese men by law.

There was nothing Chinese about it, in its origins at least. The Manchu had brought it with them from the northern steppe. They insisted on its adoption as an acknowledgement of their rule. The Manchu might be masters, but they were overwhelmingly outnumbered in their newly conquered realm, never representing more than a small percentage of the population. As impressive as their achievement had already been in taking over this vast new territory, they faced major challenges in consolidating their hold.

The formula they found for doing this was a curious but effective combination of carrot and stick. On the one hand, they took great care to support their subjects' sense of patriotic Chinese pride, keeping many of the country's existing laws and institutions. The civil service exam system was as important as it had ever been. On the other hand, they drove home their mastery with such calculatedly humiliating decrees as the 'Queue Order'. This demanded that all Chinese males have their hair styled in the Manchu way on pain of death.

Many were to die in defence of their traditional Chinese hair – long, free, unrestrained and (above all) unshaved. As Philip A. Kuhn has pointed out, the sticking point was not the queue itself – Chinese men had always worn their hair long. The insult lay in the Manchu insistence that their heads should be bare from the forehead up. Traditionally, in Chinese society, criminals had been forced to have their heads shaved as a punishment. It was regarded as a shame – even something close to mutilation.

It was as important to the Chinese that they should resist what they saw as an alien and essentially barbaric order as it was to the Qing authorities that they should obey. In fairness, those comparatively few officials who chose to take this proclamation literally and carry out massacres of non-compliant males seem largely to have been Chinese defectors desperate to show their loyalty to the new regime. This was the zeal of the convert – or, perhaps, the guilty resentment of the turncoat. But the Manchu, under the leadership of Shunzhi's regent, Prince Rui, or Dorgon (1612–50), did not flinch from the widespread use of force.

MANY WERE TO DIE IN DEFENCE OF THEIR TRADITIONAL CHINESE HAIR – LONG, FREE, UNRESTRAINED AND (ABOVE ALL) UNSHAVED

TWICE A TRAITOR

GENERAL WU SANGUI (1612–78) rose high under the Ming in the 1630s, fighting bravely against advancing Manchu forces. In 1644, however, seeing that all was up with the old regime, he faced a choice between siding with the invaders or with homegrown Chinese rebels. In the event, he threw in his lot with Dorgon and the Qing and helped them put down rebel resistance in Beijing.

In the years that followed, Wu became a trusted henchman of the Qing, and a tireless, often brutal, enforcer of their rule. After crushing one peasant uprising in Shanxi, to the north, he was sent to the southwest to suppress another in Sichuan, and ultimately given charge of Yunnan and Guizhou under the Qing. Two other Chinese leaders were granted similar 'feudatory' status in other southern regions, remote from Beijing: Shang Kexi (1604–76) in Guangdong, in the far south, and Geng Jingzhong in Fujian, in the country's southeastern corner.

The concentration of so much power in the hands of three individuals (and foreign individuals at that) was not ideal from the Manchu's point of view. It had been forced on them by the demands of occupying a country in which they were badly outnumbered. Naturally enough, as the Kangxi Emperor felt his hold on China strengthening in the 1670s, he took steps to call them to account, recalling them to other posts in Manchuria. Led, it seems, by Wu Sangui, now a traitor for a second time, they rebelled together in 1673 in what became known as the Revolt of the Three Feudatories. They were finally defeated, but it took eight years.

The reign of the Kangxi Emperor (1654–1722), from 1661, was a time of consolidation for the Qing. But if he brought peace to China, it was by some rough and ready means. Insurrections along the northern border were cruelly put down and Kangxi moved local populations in the region around like pawns to create a demographic balance more to his liking. The Dzungar people, originally Mongols, proved a particular challenge, until their armies were virtually wiped out by the Qing in 1696.

Below: The Kangxi Emperor's consort – believed to be his third empress, Xiao Yi Ren. She had charge of all his 56 children.

FROM SUCCESS TO SUCCESSION STRUGGLE

Kangxi's 40 consorts bore him 56 children, 36 of them sons, of whom 24 survived. His family life, accordingly, was a succession struggle waiting to happen, although he openly favoured his second son, Yinreng (1674–1725). Kangxi awarded Yinreng the status of Crown Prince when he was only an infant, and remained close to him from that time on – much more so than was customary in an elite household of that time. As he grew, though, Yinreng alienated his father with his sexual incontinence and general dissipation; it was said that he bought slave children to abuse. Just as bad in the imperial scheme was the fact that he had sexual relations with one of his father's concubines – an act of incest under Chinese law.

Yinreng was thrown into prison, only to be released when it emerged that his envious brother Yinzhi (1672–1735) had been casting spells on him. A few years later, though, as Yinreng persisted in his immoral ways, his father decided that his eighth son, Yinzhen (1678–1735), should be his heir as Yongzheng Emperor. Yinzhen duly succeeded 1723, although the fight to assert his authority over his brother-princes was to occupy him for the first few years of his reign.

The bitter confusion over Yinzhen's succession seems to have left its mark: his was a conspicuously authoritarian reign. Even for an imperial monarch, Yinzhen was unusually controlling. Not only did he make a point of underlining his choice of his fourth son Hongli (1711–99) as his heir, but also he is said to have made his third son, Hongshi (1704–27), commit suicide to assure his smooth succession. Like his distant predecessor Shihuangdi, Yinzhen appears to have hoped that such a succession might never be necessary, devoting much energy to the quest for an immortality elixir. Once again, ironically, this may actually have helped to hasten his death.

Above: Prince Yinzhi's bitterness was notorious – but also understandable, given his father's favouring of his younger half-brother Yinreng.

EXPANSIONISM AND EXPENSE

As Qianlong Emperor from 1735, Hongli took Qing China to its highest renown and its greatest geographical extent. Once again, however, the path to glory would be bloody. The great achievement of the era, for China, was the domestication of large parts of its wild west, in the steppes of Xinjiang and other frontier zones. The nomadic tribes defeated, and confined to clearly demarcated areas of pastureland, Chinese colonists were brought in to bring the country under cultivation. Towns were founded and laws and currency introduced.

Despite efforts to increase prosperity and stability, agricultural production rose slowly and was at best erratic given frequent droughts; intensive and expensive policing was required to keep rebellious tribes in check. Even when they were not actively in revolt, local people were passively resistant to Qing rule.

Formed over generations, their ties of kinship and commerce alike were with Central Asia and they were slow to look south and east to China.

Below: Heshen's depredations on state coffers were the stuff of real-life legend.

KLEPTOCRAT IN CHIEF

Heshen (1750–99), the emperor's chief minister, was the most corrupt official in Chinese history. Not only did he hawk the functions of the state for bribes, but also he did this openly, completely unabashed, and with no sign of disapproval from his master. Qianlong looked the other way while he levied taxes essentially on his own behalf, amassing a colossal personal fortune from 'state' funds.

Heshen had started in Qianlong's service as a bodyguard about the palace, but rumours were rife that he had attended the emperor much more closely in his bed. Then as now, in China as elsewhere, the suggestion of homosexuality was often levelled as a demeaning smear. But, it was wondered, what otherwise would account for Qianlong's loyalty to a man so demonstrably unfit for his official status?

By the time Heshen was through, he had helped himself to more than 1000 million taels, it is calculated – some 15 times the annual income of the Chinese state. He had more houses than could readily be counted across some 32 sq km (12.35 sq miles) of land, and huge reserves of artworks, jewellery and gold. Naturally enough, his underlings were eager to follow his example. Institutions of every kind were bled by their supposed custodians; the infrastructure of the entire empire – from roads and canals to public buildings – went to ruin as money for maintenance and new construction was systematically diverted.

Qianlong, who was so exacting – cruel, even – in other areas, turned a deaf ear to complaints. Only after the emperor's death in 1799 was Heshen brought to justice by his successor. Jiaqing lost no time in arresting his father's favourite and confiscating his ill-gotten wealth, and then had him executed for his crimes.

Below: Gao Tianxi, who died in 1758, was a Dzungar who'd served as a soldier in the emperor's army.

'NO MERCY'

THE DZUNGAR HAD CAUSED trouble before on China's northwestern frontier, but despite severe punishment, they had bounced back. By the 1750s, they were once more beginning to kick against Qing rule. Rallying behind the charismatic chieftain Amursana, resolute action by Beijing was clearly called for. Emperor Qianlong was surely correct in his conclusion that they were likely to remain persistent offenders. His solution – their complete 'extermination' – was more questionable.

'No mercy' was to be shown, the emperor insisted. The entire Dzungar people were to be exterminated; officers refusing to comply suffered punishment themselves. Their menfolk having been slaughtered, the women and children were to be shared out among the soldiery as slaves. In the event, anything from 480,000 to 800,000 people were to die. While most were killed in the fighting, and the programme of massacres that quickly followed, many thousands died of smallpox brought unwittingly by the invaders. The Dzungar Genocide provides insight into the sort of racist rationalization that allows atrocities first to be conceived of and then committed by men who aren't actually monsters. Qianlong could only justify his actions in Confucian terms by convincing himself that the Dzungar were in some sense not fully human. Once he had persuaded himself of this, his decision was quite easy. Emptied of these 'barbarians', their territory could be colonized by more tractable Chinese settlers.

BATAVIAN VICTIMS

TODAY, IN JUST ABOUT every part of the world, we see representatives of that vast but scattered diaspora of Overseas Chinese, which, although long established in foreign countries, still maintains close emotional and economic ties with the mother country. This community did not appear overnight, but grew slowly over centuries, starting in Southeast Asia and the East Indies.

The first few travelled as traders up and down the region's coasts, while subsequent waves went en masse as migrant workers. Many found employment with European colonists in the Spice Islands. Hence the many thousands to be found by the early 18th century in the Dutch settlement of Batavia – now Jakarta, capital of Indonesia, on the coast of Java. Most were working in sugar mills and on the associated plantations. Others helped to grow or harvest rice or teak or to mine tin.

By the 1730s, the sheer number of ethnic Chinese was starting to unsettle the Dutch colonists on the ground. A collapse of sugar prices had hit Batavia hard. Resentment against the Chinese rose steadily, not just among the European population but also among the native Javans, now competing with the Chinese for scarce work.

Tempers flared with the colonial authorities' imposition of a registration scheme for Chinese immigrants. In October 1740, rioting broke out in Chinese districts around Batavia. In one memorable night of near-war, 50 Dutch soldiers were killed, and the authorities determined to crack down. This was done with the cooperation of the European settlers who, in the days that followed, conducted what amounted to a pogrom. 'I myself had to join in', one German carpenter reported,

And because I knew that my neighbour had a fat pig, I wanted to get it and take it to my house. When the master carpenter saw this, he hit me and said I should kill the Chinese first, and not rob him. So, lacking a weapon, I quickly took a rice pounder, a long piece of wood as thick as an arm, and with it beat my neighbour, with whom I had often sat drinking, to death.... Once I had killed him, I went to his room, where I found a pistol, and took it and a number of bullets for it as well. I went on and shot everyone I met. Once I had killed two or three, I was so accustomed to the butchery, and had few feelings of remorse about it. It didn't matter whether I killed a Chinese or a dog.

More than 10,000 Chinese are believed to

have been killed in all. Therefore, even as imperial China was playing the oppressor on its inland frontiers, its emigrant men and women were being bullied and exploited. This was a foretaste of what was to come as contact developed and grew with the Western powers – so much better equipped and armed than its own forces were.

Below: The Chinese quarter of Batavia, Java, goes up in flames as the slaughter continues in the streets outside.

Above: White Lotus adherents followed the Mother Goddess Wusheng Laomu, whose symbol we see here.

Opposite: The Emperor Qianlong on horseback.

The people in China itself were not enamoured of their emperor. The degree of their disaffection is evident in the new popularity of the White Lotus sect. A branch of Chinese Buddhism, this movement found thousands of new adherents in the reign of Qianlong in the late 18th century.

Although it had not been of great significance since the Yuan era, it had never quite gone away. It had always enjoyed upsurges in times of economic hardship and other adversities and drawn strength from a prevailing sense that the people's official protectors were uncaring and corrupt. It was also, paradoxically, empowered by the hostility of the Qing, whose general repressiveness effectively forced religious mystics to make common cause with political dissidents and criminals.

WOMEN OF WAR

One token of White Lotus' radicalism was the feminized feel it always had, starting with the movement's veneration of Wusheng Laomu, the Great Mother Goddess. It was she, White Lotus preachers promised, who would, through a series of cleansing catastrophes (plagues, floods, famines), prepare the world for complete renewal with the advent of the Maitreya Buddha. The sect was also transgressive in its wider attitudes to women. Not only were the sexes allowed to worship and fraternize together with a freedom unprecedented in Chinese tradition, but also women were often allowed to play a leading role.

Wang Cong'er (1777–97), from Xiangyang, was said to have been radicalized by the killing of her husband by the Qing. She became a brave and resourceful guerrilla leader, skilled in hand-to-hand combat. Cornered in the mountains of Hubei province by a pursuing imperial army, she leapt heroically to her death rather than be taken captive. The life of her comrade, Wang Nangxian (1778–98), followed a broadly similar trajectory – even to her suicide. These may have been real women, but they were also semi-mythic martyr figures. While Wang Cong'er and Wang Nangxian represented the political resistance of their people, they also served as symbols. Their femininity seemed to connect them to the earth and to express in them the suffering

WRITING WRONGS

SUCCESSIVE EMPERORS, MOST NOTORIOUSLY Shihuangdi, Hongwu and Yongle, had been uncomfortable with China's intellectuals. They had been particularly touchy about historical scholarship that drew unwanted attention to the sometimes messy circumstances of their ascent.

As outnumbered foreigners seeking to stamp their authority on an enormous and ancient empire, the Qing emperors were understandably uneasy. What became known as the 'Literary Inquisition' became institutionalized – and under Qianlong an ever-present part of Chinese life. The strictness of this censorship prompted writers to be more oblique in their criticisms of the status quo, which only encouraged Qing officials in their paranoia.

The very mention of their Ming predecessors could be seen as a reproach, as could the incautious use of the character 'qing', which simply meant 'clear' or 'bright'. In 1755, Hu Zonghao, a Hunan official, wrote an innocent lyric contrasting meanings that were misty (or murky), zhuo, and those that were qing, so clear and bright. This meant the association in the same line of the name Qing and the concepts of unclarity and by extension grubbiness and dirt. Hu and his whole family were beheaded on the Qianlong emperor's orders.

'Red is the only true colour for peonies,' wrote Cai Xian (1697–1767) in what came to be seen as a treasonous poetic flight. Zhu, the word he used for 'red', was also the family name of the Ming emperors. Was he saying that they were the only real rulers, and that the Manchu were by implication interlopers? That was the official reading. Cai Xian too paid for his poetic licence with his life.

While it is the savagery of this censorship that most immediately appals, the cultural cost was incalculably high as well. In the last 20 years of Qianlong's reign, an estimated 150,000 books were destroyed, representing the loss of more than 3000 distinct texts.

of the agrarian peasantry as a whole – much like the legendary 'Poor Old Woman', Kathleen Ni Houlihan, did for the Irish nationalists of the 19th century.

KOWTOW CONTRETEMPS

George, Earl Macartney (1737–1806), dispatched to Beijing to discuss the opening of trade links between Britain and China in 1792, was sent on his way with a dusty answer. Notoriously, he had refused to 'kowtow'. Visitors in the presence of the emperor were supposed to perform an elaborate ritual of obeisance. The full kowtow involved the guest getting down into a kneeling position, from which he then bent down and bumped his forehead against the floor nine times.

Britain was at the time a relatively minor imperial power (and had lost its American colonies only a decade previously).

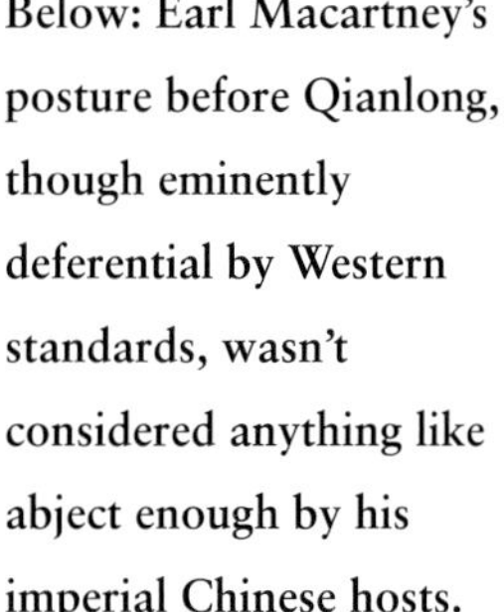

Below: Earl Macartney's posture before Qianlong, though eminently deferential by Western standards, wasn't considered anything like abject enough by his imperial Chinese hosts.

Above: Between agrarian unrest in the provinces and assassination attempts at court, Jiaqing faced one challenge after another throughout his reign.

Even so, no delegate of King George III (1738–1820) could imagine abasing himself (or his nation) so utterly in the presence of a foreign head of state. Not, at least, without some serious sign of reciprocity. Earl Macartney duly produced a portrait of his king. If a senior Chinese official would kowtow to him – or to his picture at least – then he would do the same for Qianlong. Horror-struck by this suggestion, the emperor and his advisers flatly refused. The meeting broke down and Macartney's mission left empty-handed. It is hard to say how far the 'kowtow' question had caused the diplomatic deadlock and how far it had been a symptom of the deeper cultural incomprehension that made it inevitable.

White racism aside, it was never realistic to expect the delegate of a global trading partner to show Qianlong the sort of reverence he could expect from the representatives of regional client-states. But then he wasn't interested in realism of that kind. Experiences like this only helped drive home the conviction in the Qing that their empire would be better off without the outside world.

DOMESTIC DANGERS

Not all was well at home, although there was stability at the top – for a few years, at least. In 1796, Qianlong officially abdicated. Not because of any crisis: he simply felt that it would have been unfilial of him to reign for longer than his grandfather had done. The Jiaqing Emperor (1760–1820) was little more than a figurehead for the first three years of his reign: Qianlong carried on directing things behind the scenes. In 1799, however, when his father died, Jiaqing stepped out from his shadow. He was resolute in pursuing what he regarded as his duties, chief among which was restoring order in his realm.

Jiaqing was not short of challenges. Corruption had been rife, with Qianlong's tacit blessing. Jiaqing prosecuted Heshen and other egregiously venal officials. But there were other, deadlier, threats as well. The emperor only narrowly escaped with his life after a couple of serious assassination attempts – the first in 1803; the second ten years later.

The shocking headline here was that the conspiracies against Jiaqing had been led by his own envious brothers, who were duly executed, and by his wider kinship group, who were sent into exile in their hundreds. The less sensational, but more serious, story was that these family intrigues were the froth atop a wider and much deeper social ferment: agrarian unrest was an almost constant feature of Jiaqing's reign.

Below: The future Daoguang Emperor sees off the threat to his father Jiaqing when he is attacked by rivals from his wider family.

FROM THE *TIANDIHUI* TO THE TRIADS

The White Lotus sect, which had not yet been completely quelled, was one of several semi-religious, semi-political

societies in China at this time. Another was the *Tiandihui* ('Society of Heaven and Earth'). As we saw with the White Lotus, such cults found fertile ground for growth in impoverished rural China in times of general discontent. They were driven in the first instance by the desire for something more; not just more materially rewarding, but more spiritually fulfilling too. The extent of their aspiration is indicated by the name of one of the *Tiandihui's* offshoots, the *Sanhehui*, or 'Three Harmonies' Society'. As its name, and its emblem, a simple triangle, suggested, it sought a balanced and benevolent three-way relationship between heaven, earth and humanity.

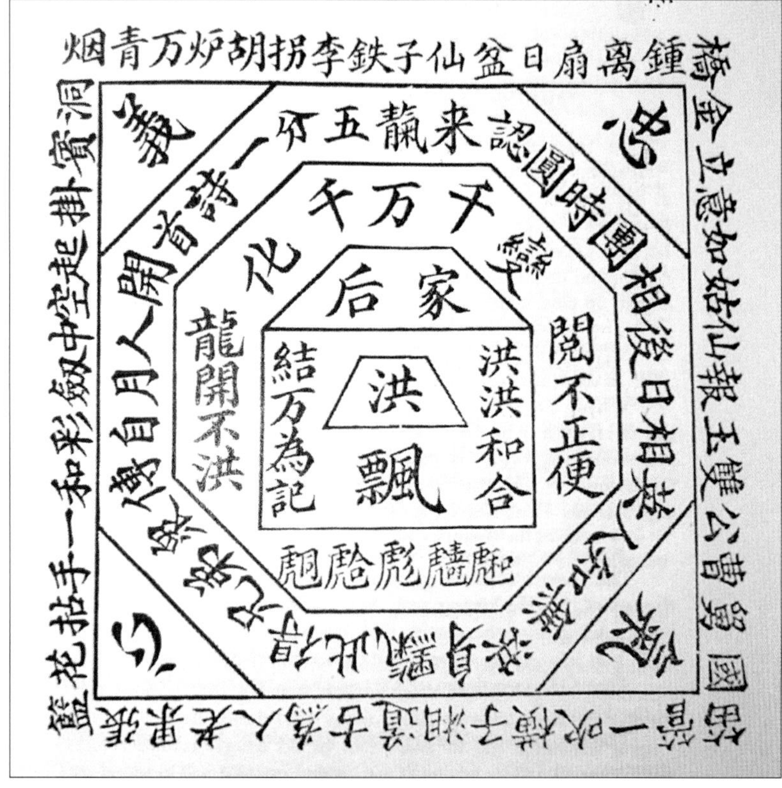

Above: The seal of the Society of Heaven and Earth (*Tiandihui*).

The rise of such groups was further fostered by the crudely disciplinarian attitude of the authorities. Not only did their repressive policies produce a resentful backlash in the countryside, but also their blanket intolerance had the effect of bracketing together religious heterodoxy, political dissidence and regular criminality into an unholy trinity of opposition. So the man or woman who hankered after mystic meaning was, automatically, a rebel against the state as well, just as the person who stole a pig was not just a thief but a social saboteur.

THEIR RISE WAS FURTHER FOSTERED BY THE CRUDELY DISCIPLINARIAN ATTITUDE OF THE AUTHORITIES.

This outlaw status came to mark the *Tiandihui* more and more, not just in official eyes but in those of their adherents too. It would take until the 20th century, and the collapse of the Qing, but the eventual transition of the 'Three Harmonies' group into

'THE CHINESE LADY'

In October 1834, a merchant ship, the *Howard*, sailed into New York Harbour, laden with the treasures of the East. Along with Chinese luxuries such as silk, tea, porcelain, pictures and lacquered wooden furniture imported by brothers Nathaniel and Frederick Carne was a real, live human woman: Afong Moy.

Afong Moy had been given that name for English-speaking ease – that we don't know her Chinese name sums up her situation. Nor, for that matter, do we know anything of her antecedents – although the Carne brothers put out press releases about her supposed royal lineage.

Afong Moy's arrival certainly caused a stir. The Carne brothers printed tickets so New Yorkers could come and see her sipping tea in a specially set-up room draped with silks and furnished in a stagey Chinese style. Her four-inch feet were an object of especial fascination. Aware of this, she held them up obligingly.

Ominously, Afong Moy had disappeared from view by the 1850s. We don't know what happened to her, but she had certainly been forgotten. She was only the first of a series of her countrypeople who were to be displayed as 'living statues' in American stores as advertisements for Chinese products such as tea.

UNPRECEDENTED ATTRACTION!!

AFONG MOY,

THE CHINESE LADY,

FOR TWO DAYS ONLY,

Friday and Saturday, 19th and 20th May,

At the Musical Fund Hall, each Evening, at 8 o'clock. Admittance, 50 cents; Children, half price.

AFONG MOY is a native of Canton city, about sixteen years of age, mild and engaging in her manners; addresses the visitors in English and Chinese, and occasionally WALKS BEFORE THE COMPANY, so as to afford an opportunity of observing her

ASTONISHING LITTLE FEET!

For which the Chinese Ladies are so remarkable. Afong's feet are FOUR INCHES and an eighth in length, being about the size of an infant's of one year old. She will be richly dressed in

THE CHINESE COSTUME

And in order to give the audience an idea of the Language and Cadence of her country, she will sing

A CHINESE SONG.

AFONG MOY is at present under the care of the Lady of the conductor of the exhibition, and is making rapid progress in acquiring the English language. Various Chinese curiosities will be shown and explained to the Company, and every pains taken to satisfy the curious, as to the manners and customs of these singular people.

She was brought to this country by Captain Obear, of the ship Washington, under a heavy guarantee to return her to her parents in two years, and is now on her way to New York, for that purpose, to embark for Canton in the 'Mary Ballard,' just arrived from China. The conductor of the exhibition, consequently, can remain but a very short time in the city; and confidently hopes that the same liberal patronage shown in other cities will not be withheld in this, after traveling so many thousand miles to solicit the favor.

☞A small quantity of beautiful Chinese Paintings, on rice paper, for sale.

May 18

Right: Afong Moy was exhibited as an exotic curiosity for an American audience which could never regard her as truly real.

the Triad gangster movement was indicative of the trend in the movement as a whole.

A TRAFFIC IN TRAGEDY

The greatest menaces to Chinese society seemed to be coming into the country from outside. Jiaqing banned the proselytization of Christianity, which was being preached by Catholic missionaries, several of whom he had put to death for defying his decrees. Across most of China, though, the opium of the people appeared to be opium itself.

The problem was not new. Opium had officially been outlawed in 1729, and the rules further tightened in 1799. 'Opium has a very violent effect,' an imperial statement had noted. 'When an addict smokes it, it rapidly makes him extremely excited and capable of doing anything he pleases. But before long, it kills him. Opium is a poison, undermining our good customs and morality.' Despite such warnings, the rate of opium use had continued to soar. By the time Jiaqing's successor the Daoguang Emperor (1782–1850) had ascended the throne, the number of addicts was approaching six million.

British merchants had enabled the addiction. Chinese tea, silk and ceramics were in great demand in Europe, and the East India Company had long paid for these in silver. There was a never-ending demand for this metal in China's imperial

Below: Westerners saw opium as an oriental scourge, but the Chinese were its victims – and the English were overwhelmingly to blame.

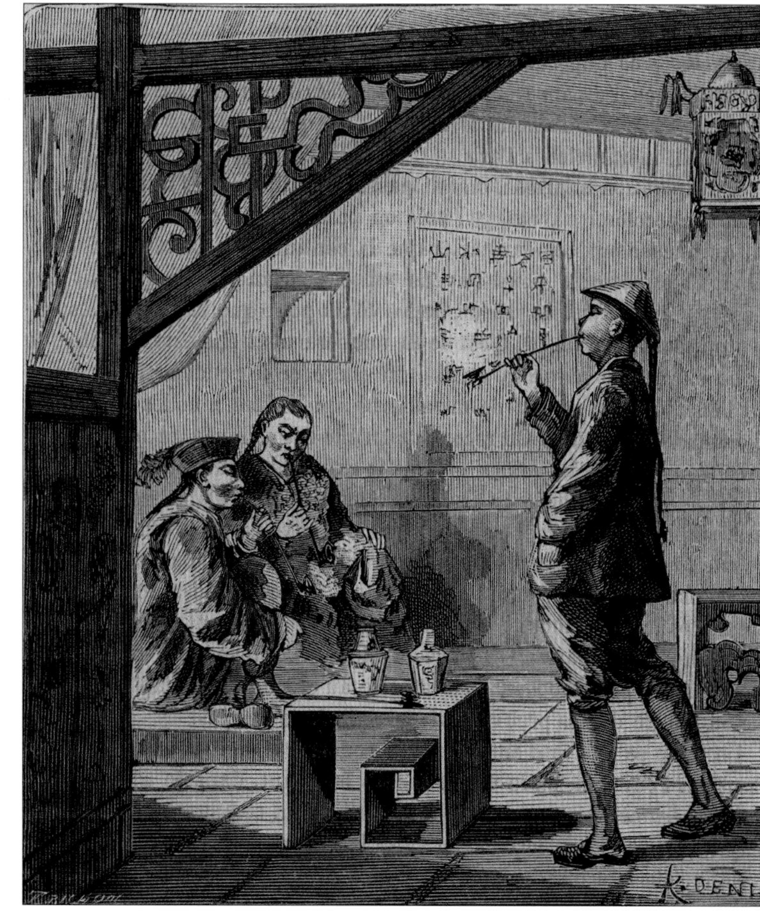

Above: The Emperor Daoguang did his best to rid China of opium, but met with obdurate resistance from British merchants, backed by the British state.

workshops, and so the crown insisted on payment in this form. British traders had at first bought their silver from European sources, but once the American colonies had gained their independence, the price had risen steeply. Why not get the silver to buy goods from China from the Chinese themselves – even if that meant bending a few rules?

Opium was the answer; it was a high-value product, and easily transportable. The poppies from which it was extracted could be grown over considerable areas of India, where they could be tended and harvested by cheap labour.

That opium was illegal in China was an inconvenience, but British merchants cleared their consciences by dealing with independent agencies – or smugglers. Soon opium was being shipped into China in considerable quantities. In 1729, 200 chests had been brought in; the figure for 1828 was 13,131.

As the opium streamed in, the silver streamed out: such was China's addiction to opium that its normal exports could not meet the cost. Between 1829 and 1840, there was a trade deficit of 45 million silver dollars and the economy was clearly heading for collapse.

KICKING THE HABIT

In 1836, Daoguang called for a crackdown on opium use, and set his special envoy, Lin Zexu (1785–1850), to implement this. Lin Zexu embarked on a programme of public education: he ordered that opium and pipes should be handed in to the authorities and had addicts taken into sanatoriums for what we might call 'rehab'. He tried his best to address the import trade. Since Guangzhou was the only port in which foreign vessels were allowed, it was relatively easy to stop the supply: the difficulty was in dealing with the British.

First, Lin Zexu wrote a letter to Queen Victoria (1819–1901):

Let us ask, where is your conscience? I have heard that the smoking of opium is very strictly forbidden by your country; that is because the harm caused by opium is clearly understood. Since it is not permitted to do harm to your own country, then even less should you let it be passed on to the harm of other countries how much less to China! Of all that China exports to foreign countries, there is not a single thing which is not beneficial to people.

No reply being received (it seems unlikely that his missive had got anywhere near the British monarch), Lin Zexu moved to more direct action. On 5 May 1839, his men stepped in to seize the 20,000 crates British merchants held in the warehouses that lined the harbour at Guangzhou. They tipped the 1250 tons of opium they found into ditches and doused them with water, lime and salt before draining the whole mess into the South China Sea.

That the British traders made no protest came as an agreeable surprise to Lin Zexu. It should not have done, however: according to the trading regulations of the time, the government was obliged to compensate merchants in full for any losses of this kind. Rather than any sudden access of conscience, it had been this fact – confirmed by Britain's Chief Superintendent of Trade in China, Captain Charles Elliot (1801–75) – that had finally persuaded the merchants to hand over their opium. They were,

Below: Lin Zexu confiscates the opium held in warehouses in Guangzhou. In the eyes of the British, this was an act of war.

they realized, in a no-lose situation: they could be paid for their product without the trouble of putting it on the market.

THE FIGHT FOR FREE TRADE

All of this illustrates the lengths to which the British government was prepared to go to uphold the principle of free trade. Disdainful of sentimentalist appeals to humanitarianism or to the wider good, they saw any sort of interference in business or commerce as unethical in itself.

Consequently, the view in London was that Lin Zexu had stolen British property and that the Chinese should be made to pay for it, by force if necessary. Far from showing any penitence, however, the imperial authorities only compounded their offence by turning back foreign shipping from Guangzhou. Captain Charles Elliot and his cousin, Admiral George Elliot (1784–1863), were placed in charge of a punitive expedition. Sixteen warships were dispatched, with 4000 soldiers on board; four modern steamships, temporarily equipped with weapons, went

Below: The First Opium War (1839–42). British warships sink Chinese vessels off Guangzhou in the Second Battle of Chuenpi, 7 January 1841.

Above: The Treaty of Nanjing (1842) was very much written by the victors. China was all but enslaved to British trading interests.

along as well. In November 1839, at the First Battle of Chuenpi, this British fleet engaged with the Chinese for the first time off Guangzhou Harbour.

A series of minor skirmishes led to the first major blow, when the Chinese sent burning rafts drifting towards the British vessels. This was stirring stuff, reminiscent of the Red Cliffs triumph of Liu Bei and Sun Quan. But the superiority of Western military technology was underscored only too clearly when the British destroyed 71 war junks and seized 60 coastal batteries. In the months that followed, they strengthened their hold on the mouth of the Pearl River and the coast around Guangzhou, both by land and sea, before shifting their attention further north.

COERCED COMMERCE

In 1842, the British smashed another Chinese war fleet off Shanghai, before seizing that city and making inroads up the Yangtze. The Chinese were powerless to resist: along with military disaster, there were thousands of civilian casualties. It was a terrible humiliation for the descendant of a dynasty of Manchu warriors to undergo, but the Qing emperor was finally forced to sue for peace.

On 29 August 1842, the victors of the First Opium War dictated the terms of the Treaty of Nanjing. Hong Kong and several adjacent islands were to be ceded to the British. Their people would not be subject to Chinese law. In addition, China had to open the ports of Shanghai, Xiamen, Ningbo, Fuzhou and Guangzhou to trade, and agree to 'most favoured nation' status for Great Britain. Any privilege granted by China to any other country would automatically apply to Britain too. Moreover, the great principle for which Britain had gone to war was at last upheld: the trade in opium was to be resumed. This was the first of a series of what historians call – for obvious reasons – 'unequal treaties' imposed on Asian rulers by Western powers.

HARD FEELINGS

China was forced to negotiate similar treaties with the USA and France, in which the right for those countries to have their own hospitals, churches and cemeteries was incorporated and the prohibition on the Catholic Church removed. For Christian missionaries, the 400 million Chinese living in ignorance of Christ's Gospel represented an enormous opportunity as well as an enormous challenge.

Below: A fatherly-looking missionary hands out tracts to grateful heathens. An idealized view of Christian evangelism in the East.

They were to find it an uphill struggle, however; not just because the vast majority of Chinese were happy with their age-old faiths but also because Christianity was now associated with Western interference. The foreigners saw China as a sink into which they could pour their opium for astronomical profits, and a pool of labour for work abroad in slave-like conditions. 'Coolies' were shipped to work on the plantations of British India and, in the 1860s, to build the western section of the Transcontinental Railroad in the United States.

Through Daoguang's last years as emperor and, from 1850, the early reign of his son Xianfeng (1831–61), popular resentment grew and grew. There was resentment both against the Qing for seemingly selling out their country so ignominiously and against the foreigners, of whom the missionaries were the most visible.

A series of attacks took place and in 1857 a French missionary was killed. This was the perfect pretext for intervention, Paris felt. Britain was at the same time smarting – or pretending to – over the detention of a Chinese ship caught smuggling, on the grounds that it had recently been registered as a British vessel. The Union Jack had thus supposedly been insulted, so Britain was ready for joint action with France. The real object of both powers, of course, was to wring further concessions from a helpless China.

A SERIES OF ATTACKS TOOK PLACE AND IN 1857 A FRENCH MISSIONARY WAS KILLED.

HOSTILITIES RENEWED

Thus began the Second Opium War. By the end of 1857, the allies had taken Guangzhou; they then marched their troops northwards as though to threaten Beijing. The hint was enough; in July 1858, the Xianfeng Emperor (1831–61) agreed to the Treaty of Tientsin (Tianjin) with Britain, France and the United States. Russia pushed for its own treaty in its turn. Permanent diplomatic representations in Beijing; payments of compensation; 11 new 'treaty ports' to be opened for trade; access to the interior; rights of navigation on the Yangtse River; a five per cent import duty on goods; the list of stipulations went on and on.

The war was not over, however. When, in 1860, it became clear that Beijing was dragging its feet over implementation, the allies brought in almost 20,000 men and more than 200 ships by

way of reinforcement. In a panic, the emperor fled Beijing and the allies moved into the city, burning and looting. As if to outdo his famous father, who had stripped the Parthenon in Athens of its iconic marble frieze, the Earl of Elgin (1811–63) ordered the systematic destruction of the emperor's exquisite Summer Palace.

The emperor had no choice but to acknowledge the Treaty of Tientsin, to which were now added the Beijing Conventions. These included still more reparations, the complete removal of duties on all foreign textiles and the ceding to Britain of the

Opposite: The Second Opium War. British and French troops combine to capture Guangzhou, December 1857.
Below: One of innumerable battles fought during the Nian Rebellion (1851–68).

THE NIAN REBELLION

THE OPIUM WARS MAY have been fought predominantly round China's southern coasts, but their effects spilled across the empire as a whole – just as the Yellow River's waters spilled across vast tracts of central Chinese countryside. A particularly bad bout of flooding in 1851 left huge areas of land under water, and claimed many thousands of human lives.

The flood was catastrophic, as was the failure of the authorities to respond effectively, bankrupted as they had been by their hostilities with the West. As before, a peasantry that felt it had lost just about everything found inspiration in a vague and informal threefold creed combining religious mysticism with political rebellion and brigandage.

The insurrection went on for the best part of 20 years, and although it was finally put down by the Qing in 1868, this was at disastrous economic and human cost. More than 100,000 people are believed to have been killed, while a ruling dynasty already severely stretched by the demands of dealing with the Opium Wars and the Taiping Rebellion was driven even further into decline.

THE HEAVENLY KINGDOM

THE GRAND NARRATIVE OF Chinese history in the middle decades of the 19th century is that of the struggle to fend off the foreign powers. Against that background, the Taiping Rebellion may be no more than incidental – yet more than 20 million people were to be killed. There was a foreign aspect to this great uprising in the south of China too, since it involved a form of Christianity. It all started in Guangdong, outside Guangzhou. Hong Xiuquan (1814–64), a young man who had several times failed his exams for the civil service, happened to hear a Chinese Protestant pastor preaching. Converting to Christianity himself, Hong Xiuquan

Above: The Taiping Rebellion cost more than 20 million lives.

Kowloon peninsula on the mainland near Hong Kong. Russia, meanwhile, was given parts of Manchuria, thereby gaining access to the Sea of Japan.

REPRESSION AND REACTION

The Second Opium War was perhaps the high-water mark for 19th-century 'gunboat' diplomacy. It ended with China carved up into convenient tranches for colonial exploitation. Russia had the north; France the south; Great Britain had the centre, and Germany and Japan had the east.

Some sort of backlash was inevitable: when it came it was once again directed at the missionaries who were the most visible promptly re-made the religion in his own way: he saw a series of visions that revealed that he was himself the son of God, younger brother to Jesus Christ. He wrote an extra 'Taiping Testament' for the Bible, and created an elaborate administrative system for his paramilitary church. He forbade opium, alcohol and tobacco and outlawed private property. He accorded equal rights to women, although he demanded strict segregation of the sexes, even for the married (they would be reunited in heaven, husbands and wives were reassured).

A poor, disaffected populace flocked to follow this extraordinarily charismatic man, who in 1851 proclaimed the 'Heavenly Kingdom of Universal Peace'. In reality, he brought not peace but the sword – indeed he had two giant blades specially forged for executing the 'vicious'. These included anyone who did not embrace his brand of Christianity: Buddhists, Taoists and Confucians. His disciples, taking their cue from him, committed atrocities as, in an army many hundreds of thousands strong, they wove their way across the interior of southern and central China.

After a series of terrible battles against government troops, the Taiping took Nanjing in 1853, making it the centre of an extensive kingdom. In the end, the movement ran out of energy. Its leader spent more and more time with his rumoured 88 concubines, and the supply of converts started to dry up. When, in 1860, the still expanding empire threatened Shanghai, that city's foreign community was alarmed. An Anglo-American force came to the assistance of the imperial army, and the rebels were gradually driven back. In 1864, the Chinese vanquished the Taiping once and for all.

representatives of foreign power. In 1870, Tientsin erupted in outrage at rumours that nuns had been abusing Chinese orphans in secret rites. A jittery French consul only made matters worse when he ordered shots to be fired into the mob. In a fury, the people rose up and killed him, before rampaging around the city destroying mission stations and churches and massacring 188 other foreigners. The Western powers reacted ruthlessly: China was forced to execute 18 suspects, pay yet more reparations and issue an official apology.

Colonialism had come to China. Not in the obvious, classic sense, perhaps: the vast majority of the population, in their rural villages, never saw a foreigner. In the treaty ports, however, a Western style of urban living was developing within those concession districts

where foreigners enjoyed self-government, and in places like Hong Kong, where Chinese sovereignty had been lifted. They had their own sanitation systems, hospitals, schools, libraries and newspapers.

Very gradually, their tastes and attitudes began to seep into the consciousness of surrounding Chinese communities, influencing everything from food preferences to ideas on the emancipation of women. Confucian modernizers, open to the West, precipitated the decline of traditional values. At the same time, however, they may have helped prepare the way for China's ultimate transition to the status of world power.

Above: Rioters in Tientsin massacred foreign missionaries in 1870.

Below: The Chinese fleet came off worse in battle with the Japanese at the Yalu River (1894).

GOING BACKWARDS

For the moment, relative to the West, China appeared to be going backwards. It also seemed to be comparing unfavourably with

other Eastern powers like Japan, which was on the rise again since the Meiji Restoration (1868). Japan's army and navy had both been radically reformed and comprehensively re-armed in the modern, Western style.

China's forces had been reformed too, up to a point: its northern Beiyang fleet was largely German- and British-built

Below: The Empress Cixi ruled China from behind the scenes for several years.

CIXI ASCENDANT

XIANFENG'S SUCCESSOR, THE TONGZHI Emperor (1856–75), had come to the throne in 1861, at the height of the Taiping Rebellion. He was only five, so had to be assisted by a team of regents: eight noble lords, along with Xianfeng's widow, the real Empress Dowager Ci'an (1837–81). Tongzhi's mother, Cixi (1835–1908), had only been the late emperor's concubine, but now she managed to get herself honoured as a sort of co-Empress Dowager with Ci'an. Before anyone knew it, she was in charge.

An attempt to oust Cixi only gave her the chance to have her foremost opponents executed and the other regents pushed aside. When Tongzhi spurned the bride she had singled out for him, insisting first on marrying Xiaozheyi (1854–75) and then on making his wife his closest confidante and counsellor, Cixi intervened and had the couple separated. Tongzhi spiralled into a life of dissolution and debauchery and died (some said of syphilis) in 1875.

Tongzhi's successor, a cousin, the Guangxu Emperor (1871–1908), was another child. Naturally, Cixi saw it as her duty to steer him through his reign. Even after he officially took over his imperial duties in 1889, she remained in power behind the curtain. He came to resent this as he grew older, especially because he came to have his own vision for China, involving extensive, essentially Westernizing, reform. Cixi's response was to stage a coup. Guangxu spent the rest of his life under house arrest, although nominally he remained emperor until 1908. His death that year came just the day before the Empress Dowager's own, leading to suggestions that she had had him poisoned to prevent his resuming his reform programme after she was gone.

and boasted eight fully armoured cruisers. Even so, a crushing French victory at the Battle of Fuzhou (1884) set the tone for a disastrous Sino–French War over ownership of the northern part of Vietnam, ending in another humiliating Treaty of Tientsin in 1885. Ten years later, China's naval forces were to take another beating – this time, ignominiously, from a rival Asian nation. Japan had been bullied by the Western powers itself, after centuries of isolation, but was now modernizing and industrializing at great speed.

> CHINA'S NAVAL FORCES WERE TO TAKE ANOTHER BEATING – THIS TIME, IGNOMINIOUSLY, FROM ANOTHER ASIAN NATION.

China had been high-handed in its dealings with its smaller neighbour. The rioting by sailors of its Beiyang fleet on shore leave in Nagasaki, in 1888, does not seem to have been officially sanctioned. But Beijing's contemptuous non-response to an outbreak of violence that had ended up involving Chinese soldiers and leaving several Japanese policemen and civilians dead made it seem as if it had been.

Festering resentment flared up into open conflict in the First Sino–Japanese War of 1894–5, during which Chinese fleets were mauled at the Yalu River (1894) and Weihaiwei (1895). These two disastrous naval defeats bookended a bloody conflict that also involved the massacre of up to 20,000 Chinese soldiers and civilians in Port Arthur (Lüshunkou, Liaoning province).

UNEQUAL TREATIES, INCONSISTENT ATTITUDES

Instability in China, for which the Western powers were partly responsible, had over several decades provided a 'push' towards migration. But the number of emigrants was to rise still further with the additional 'pull' of the California Gold Rush, which got going from around 1848. A further draw, a decade later, was the construction of the Transcontinental Railroad, 1863–9, whose western sections were largely built by Chinese labourers.

Named for President Lincoln's minister in Beijing, Anson Burlingame (1820–70), the Burlingame Treaty of 1868 sought to mend some fences after the Second Opium War. It was comparatively warm in its welcome to Chinese immigrants, several thousand of whom started arriving in California and the other Western states annually. Many white Americans in those

Above: The US congressman Anson Burlingame, magnificently whiskered, presides over the signing of the treaty that would bear his name.

states were hostile to this policy from the outset, however, and were not persuaded of the economic benefits.

Their government moved swiftly to appease them, in 1875 passing the Page Act, allowing port officials to exclude Chinese women they deemed to be 'obnoxious' – likely prostitutes, so just about any young women, in other words. Most Chinese immigrants until now had been male, either single men who had come to seek their fortunes or married householders hoping to send back money to their families. There was a thriving sex trade catering to this emigrant community, and there is no doubt that abuses took place – although those who suffered were overwhelmingly the young women themselves. More widely, what amounted to a ban on Chinese women had the longer-term effect of ensuring that no deeper, more stable social roots could be put down.

Chinese men were targeted too, however. The Chinese Exclusion Act of 1882 introduced a complete moratorium on immigration for ten years. That discriminatory employers felt able to pay Chinese workers less occasioned outrage in white

Above: The Rock Springs Massacre, as represented in a US newspaper. Twenty-eight (at least) were killed, and over 70 homes were burned.

workers who insisted that this meant that the Chinese were taking jobs they should have had. Anger at this turned violent many times, notably in the Rock Springs Massacre (1885): at least 28 Chinese labourers were killed in rioting around a Wyoming mine. Two years later, at Hells Canyon, Oregon, a gang of white criminals ambushed and murdered a group of 34 Chinese gold miners, in what seems to have been in part a robbery, in part a race attack.

RACIST RESTRICTIONS

In other English-speaking countries, although Chinese labour might be needed, the actual presence of Chinese labourers was often resented. Hence the reaction to the influx of immigrants towards the end of the 19th century in the mining centres of South Africa and Australia. In South Africa's goldfields, the British authorities, having brought in more than 60,000 'coolies' under contract in the 1900s, repatriated almost all – under pressure from white voters – after 1910. This was several decades before the official introduction of apartheid by the country's Afrikaner government.

Unsurprisingly, Australia's notorious White Australia immigration policy saw keeping the Chinese out as an important priority – though here too large numbers of contract workers had previously been brought in to work the mines. It was a point of principle for Prime Minister Edmund Barton (1849–1920) that the Chinese should be seen as subhuman. 'There is no racial equality,' he maintained. 'The doctrine of equality of man was never intended to apply to the equality of the Englishman and the Chinaman.' New Zealand never did proclaim a 'Whites Only' immigration policy as such, but did in 1881 single out Chinese immigrants to pay a poll tax, and tightly restricted numbers. Four years later, Canada was to follow suit.

Above: A Chinese miner takes time out from work in Australia, c. 1900. There were some 29,000 Chinese immigrants in the country at that time.

EVOLUTIONARY ANXIETIES

The fear of economic competition and the distrust of foreigners, unfamiliar in appearance and in customs, have often been translated into more intimately felt hostility in host communities. Talk of what became known as the 'Yellow Peril' was soon widespread among the 'white' nations. Germany's Kaiser Wilhelm II (1859–1941) helped to envision this supposed menace, it has been said, after he described a dream he had had of a Buddha-like bogeyman riding on a dragon to attack the West.

The kaiser was by no means the only one to feel the fear. Along with the economic anxieties and the sense that cultural integrity was being lost went a sexual threat. The 'Chinaman' would steal, seduce or otherwise sully white womanhood, it was assumed, just as the oriental temptress would drag white husbands into sin.

This was a time when racism was tricking itself out in all sorts of pseudoscientific guises, looking to a bastardized version of Darwin's evolutionary theories to uphold what amounted to white-supremacist ideas. Serious-sounding writers like Houston

Above: A Boxer rebel awaits execution by beheading in Beijing.

Stewart Chamberlain (1855–1927) and Christian von Ehrenfels (1859–1932) spoke of the need for the white races to unite against the oriental threat – not just for their own sake, but for the world.

KNOCKING OUT THE BOXERS

It was, ironically, Wilhelm II's racial prejudice that prompted him to tell his troops to show no mercy to their enemies; to behave like Attila's historic 'Huns'. In doing so, he endowed them with their own enduring, if in its own way racist, nickname. He was addressing an expeditionary force just off to China to help suppress the Boxer Rebellion (1899–1901). So-called by the British because its participants, members of the Militia United in Righteousness, were enthusiastic in their pursuit of martial arts, this rising represented a familiar blend of religious, cultural, economic and political feeling among the Chinese people. Some adherents wore scarves and turbans in colours associated with these historic movements.

They had come in their hundreds of thousands, to the support (as they perceived it) of a Qing Dynasty they saw being pushed about in the most humiliating way by the Western powers. They were frightening in their fanatic zeal, chanting out the war-cry 'Kill the foreign devils!', and disturbing in their cultish courage and unquestioning commitment to their cause. Not only were they buoyed up by patriotic fervour but also, it seems, by the spiritual certainty that their faith made them invulnerable to Western weapons.

The Qing establishment regarded their assistance with more ambivalence, at first sending its armies out into the country to quell the rising. They had good reason to look sceptically upon the rebels: the nationalism that the Boxers espoused was sometimes ugly, with their xenophobia often finding expression in frenzied violence. In the course of their march upon Beijing, they killed more than 30,000 Chinese Christians and up to 200 missionaries, burning down churches and mission schools as they went. Local officials lent their support: in Taiyuan, Shanxi, the governor invited 45 missionaries to his residence with their families, only to have them all paraded down the streets, stripped to the waist and publicly beheaded.

As the movement gathered strength, however – and, especially, as the West made clear its contempt for China's rulers – Cixi found herself with a real dilemma. When German diplomats executed a young Boxer they had captured, and when a combined naval force sent by Britain, the United States, Russia, France, Italy, Austria-Hungary and Japan set about bombarding Tianjin's Taku forts, the assault on China's dignity was too much to bear. Cixi shifted her position, throwing the emperor's authority behind the Boxers' cause. This was politically essential,

Below: British, Japanese and US troops storm a Boxer stronghold in Beijing. But the 'Relief of Peking' was a humiliation for China as a whole.

Above: Offerings are still left at this monument to the martyrs of the 'Railway Protection Movement' in Chengdu.

perhaps, given the prevailing mood in China, but a dangerous decision, with the rebels now laying siege to the foreign legations in Beijing.

The result was that the expeditionary forces dispatched by the world's great powers were no longer just officiously 'assisting': they were essentially at war with the Chinese Empire. The Qing's inevitable defeat by the 20,000-strong invasion force – and the just-as-inevitable concessions to the West that followed – left an already weak regime still more severely compromised.

THE RAILWAY REVOLUTION

China was slowly sliding into what Lenin would later characterize as a 'revolutionary situation': strikes and popular unrest were becoming endemic. Behind the scenes, revolutionary groups were forming, although they struggled to win the backing of the general public. The 1900s saw a string of local uprisings taking place, which were all duly crushed. Now it was the turn of the middle class.

To this day, when conservative historians insist upon the 'benefits' of imperialism to the colonized countries, the construction of railways is invariably high up among the 'gifts' they list. The reality was generally more complicated. Big concessions were exacted by Western companies in China for the privilege of having them there. Meanwhile, much of the money used to build this infrastructure came from local people with savings to invest and the desire for a stake in the economic advancement of their communities.

In 1911, a government frantically casting round for ways of paying reparations agreed to in the wake of the Boxer Rebellion hit on the idea of taking railway companies under official ownership. They could then be used as security for loans from foreign banks, which might in turn be put towards the reparations. Private shareholders were naturally alarmed and, in Sichuan and Hubei provinces, where many members of the public had made investments, a 'Railway Protection Movement' was formed.

When a demonstration in Chengdu, Sichuan, was broken up by troops with the loss of more than 30 lives, the situation started spiralling into chaos. On 11 October, in Wuchang, Hubei, revolutionaries rose up and attacked the city's Qing garrison. They were joined by mutineers from the Imperial Army. Although the rebels were finally defeated by Qing forces at the Battle of Yangxia, they had held out in Wuchang's neighbouring cities of Hankou and Hanyang for many weeks. Not only did their heroism help inspire opposition elsewhere in China, but also it underlined the weakness of the regime.

The revolution appeared to be acquiring unstoppable momentum. In December, revolutionary forces in Jiangsu province took Nanjing. Here, as in Xi'an, Shaanxi, and Guangzhou, hundreds of thousands of ethnic Manchu are believed to have been slaughtered. Nanjing became the capital for a new provisional government. On 1 January, the Republic of China was proclaimed.

Below: The capture of Nanjing by revolutionary troops marked a turning point: the city became the capital of a new Republic of China.

中國工農紅軍

5

Into the Fire

The collapse of the imperial order held out the promise of democracy and progress. This promise, however, would not be kept.

They were 'listening to the telephone', townspeople said. Two human heads, suspended by their own hair, hung from the crossbeam high up on a utility pole, among the wires crisscrossing above the busy Jinan street. They swung slowly, stirred by the gentle breeze. If they weren't really listening, they were certainly speaking in their silent way: don't even dream of crossing Zhang, they said.

Opposite: Mao Zedong, Zhou Enlai and Lin Biao lead the way to victory in a celebrated painting of the Long March.

Zhang Zongchang (1881–1932) was as dangerous as he was unpleasant. Shandong's local warlord had 'the build of an elephant, the brain of a pig and the temperament of a tiger', it had been observed. His mother had been, quite literally, a witch. He had spent time as a pickpocket, bouncer, gold prospector and bandit. His reign confirmed that he had learned important lessons from all these careers. In just three years, from June 1925 to April 1928, Zhang had ransacked the province and robbed its people on an epic scale.

Along with traditional taxes on land and property, which he had hiked up again and again, Zhang had added new ones on everything from dogs to brothels, from firewood and chickens to

Above: The great might-have-been of modern Chinese history: could Sun Yat-sen have brought his country freedom and justice without mass-slaughter?

opium pipe lighters and vegetables. New charges had been levied to fund specific projects – everything from furnishing his soldiers with new shoes to commissioning a bronze statue of himself. He had also extorted money from banks and businesses, in the guise of loans. 'If figured by regular rates of taxation,' a contemporary source had estimated, the sums raised by such measures 'would exceed all taxes to be paid until 1939'.

Largely uneducated himself, Zhang's main contact with his province's institutions of secondary and higher education had been his regular recruiting raids. Bursting into classrooms and lecture halls, he and his men had dragged students from their desks and off to whatever battlefronts they had been fighting on.

Zhang's ignorance was immense and unabashed. He openly boasted of embodying the 'Three Don't Knows': he didn't know how much money he had, how many soldiers or how many concubines; he had so many of all three. But the biggest 'don't know' about Zhang was, perhaps, how had such a monster come to wield so much power?

RISING SUN

Things had promised to be different. Sun Yat-sen (1866–1925) had paid his revolutionary dues in a series of unsuccessful risings through the 1890s and 1900s. Now he had been (provisionally) elected head of state – and of an optimistic and progressive state at that, under the government of Sun's Kuomintang, or National Party of China (KMT).

The 'Three Principles' around which it set out to build its new society included: first, a sort of social welfare, with provision of food, clothing, housing and healthcare available to all; second, a commitment to democracy and freedom; and third, a strong spirit of Chinese nationhood.

If the idea of 'nationalism' has acquired some disconcerting associations since, Sun's version was explicit in rejecting any ethnic basis. Being Chinese was more about not belonging to one of that rapacious crew of foreign, Western nations that had been oppressing and pillaging China for so long. All the country's peoples – not just the majority Han but also Mongols, Manchu,

Tibetans, Uighurs and other communities – had equal claim to Chinese identity and pride.

STRANGE BEDFELLOWS

Within weeks, it had become clear that Sun would have to wait for his grander vision to be realized. Compromise would be needed in the shorter term, at least. That meant an accommodation with more left-wing revolutionaries in China – chief among these, the Communists. Sun's work in social reform and in resisting Western imperialism won fulsome praise from the Soviet leader Lenin, although their alliance seems to have been largely one of convenience on both sides.

Young idealists in China, Sun's natural supporters, were natural sympathizers with the Soviet system too. Not, perhaps, in the arcane details of its Marxist-Leninist ideology or the bewildering ins and outs of its party politicking, but in its broad-brush achievement in mobilizing the masses to overthrow the Russian Czars.

Below: Taking time out from the tumults of the Civil War, Sun Yat-sen (centre) visits the tombs of the Ming emperors.

Soviet Russia had more practical assistance to offer too. Sun himself had blessed the bringing in of Soviet advisers to shape the Kuomintang from a loose alliance of well-meaning but unworldly activists into a disciplined party run on streamlined Leninist lines. At the same time, his reliance on the educated bourgeoisie in China cautioned him against too close an association with the sort of self-consciously 'proletarian' revolution that Russia represented. These were contradictory feelings, and they undoubtedly created tensions that would flare up into open hostility later on. For the moment, though, the Kuomintang and Communists maintained a united front.

Below: The comic-opera colonel had some serious ambition: Yuan Shikai had himself made emperor for a time in 1915.

STRONGMEN IN SUPPORT

Despite the strategic backing of the Soviets, Sun needed direct support from the military to hold on to such power as he had. That meant dealing with the powerful and dictatorially minded general Yuan Shikai (1859–1916), who made the presidency the price of his cooperation. Eventually, that was not enough.

From December 1915, Yuan even reigned as Hongxian Emperor, although this imperial restoration was over within three months. Yunnan, and other southern provinces, took the opportunity to secede, and what became known as the National Protection War started. It was brought to a close by Yuan's ignominious abdication.

UNWANTED EMPEROR

No more than a toddler when his 'reign' began, Puyi (1906–67) was still some way off puberty when he was forced to abdicate. The twelfth and last Qing Emperor (ruled 1908–12), he was forced to live on as the symbol of a superannuated order. For the first few years, Puyi was a prisoner of the Chinese state, unable to leave the Forbidden City in Beijing; then, from 1924, he became a captive of the Japanese. For the following seven years, he lived in the coastal city (and Japanese concession) of Tianjin.

A spell in Manchurian exile followed, and a pantomime of power as Chief Executive of Manchukuo, a Japanese colonial territory in northeastern China. Puyi seems to have seen his coronation as 'emperor' in 1934 as the beginning of better things – both for himself and for China, which was by now deep into its bitter and destructive civil war.

Puyi's next captivity came in 1945, at the hands of the Soviet forces that now occupied Manchuria. A few years later, Puyi was returned to China, which was now under Communist control. To his great surprise, he was not executed, or even imprisoned, although he did have to undergo the challenge of learning the sort of basic tasks an emperor did not normally engage with – everything from cleaning his teeth to tying his shoelaces. He did not complain, however, and even seems to have enjoyed his work as a street sweeper and civic gardener. He led a simple life until he died aged 61.

Above: Puyi ascended the throne as a tiny boy.

INTO THE NORTH

Yuan Shikai may have been humbled, but his military comrades were undiminished in their might. They continued to hold sway, especially in north and central China. In some cases, however, they were beginning to go their own way, detaching themselves from any sort of central government and reliant on the power

LESS THAN DOGS

Passed in 1910 by the US Congress, the White-Slave Traffic Act set out to deal with a social problem that seems to have existed largely in the lurid imaginations of politicians and the public. Underpinning it emotionally, however, was a widely felt outrage at the corruption of respectable white womanhood by ethnically and ethically alien 'white slavers' operating out of China – an idea encouraged by moral purity campaigners. 'I was scarcely prepared for the sights I met at Tientsin', Jean Turner Zimmermann was to write in *The Social Menace of the Orient* (1921):

To the woman sold into a life of shame in the seaports of the Orient only one fate can come. A year or two in some dark hole, nothing to eat, vile, filthy surroundings, vermin of every kind, opium, frightful disease, 'yaws' (Oriental syphilis), torturing, tearing into the vitals of life ...

The experience, she suggested, was unbearable to the morally healthy mind. It was therefore literally maddening, leading to insanity and death.

'For every girl who reads this,' Zimmermann warned,

I want to paint a real life picture of girl slavery in the Orient. I want to tell you of one sick, starving girl in Tientsin, chained all day in the cellar of an Oriental dive, forced to the door of the hut above as the evening shadows fell, to stand stripped to the waist and beg the white, black and yellow faces of the world to come in. ...

The jumbling up of different coloured faces suggests a breaking of boundaries, an overthrow of respectable norms, just as the picture of the white girl forced to 'beg' for such degradation upsets a 'natural' hierarchy in which she should self-evidently be at the top.

'The white prostitute in China, aside from her money-making value, is less thought of by the Chinese themselves than the dog that haunts the outlying graveyards of the country and lives by gnawing the body and bones of the baby that has been left out for him.'

they drew from their soldiers' loyalty and strength. Hence came the rise of regional warlords such as Zhang Zongchang.

Sun Yat-sen was still strong in the southern provinces. In 1917, to counter what was happening in the north, he set up his own 'Constitutional Protection Junta' in Guangzhou. His intention was to mount a Northern Expedition against the generals' government and the warlords. In the end, that task was left to his successor, Chiang Kai-shek (1887–1975). Sun's longstanding protégé, Chiang appears to have done his best to continue with his mentor's work: he finally launched the Northern Expedition in 1927 at the head of a huge National Revolutionary Army (NRA).

In the event, the Expedition did not just pit him against the warlords and their forces, as always anticipated. Most, including Zhang's men, melted away after offering almost no resistance. More important was the collision course it brought him on to with the Communists. Outwardly, the Kuomintang

Below: Chiang Kai-shek may have been Sun Yat-sen's protégé but the autocratic tendencies at which this photo hints were all his own.

was still basking in the approval of the Soviets: Chiang himself was known in Moscow as the 'Red General'. Behind the scenes, though, the Chinese Nationalists were coming to feel that the Russians were trying to take over their movement.

SHANGHAI SHOWDOWN

Chiang's first major prize was the industrial city of Wuhan, in Hubei province, and the highpoint of his campaign came with the conquest of Shanghai. A great seaport, with enormous industrial facilities, it was the unofficial capital of trade unionism in China – a place where leftist activists were always going to feel at home. As if to underline this fact, trade unionists in the city rolled out a welcome mat: a general strike by 600,000 workers greeted the NRA on its arrival at the end of March 1927.

Below: The Nationalists captured a huge amount of weaponry when they took Shanghai.

Shanghai was also the most important centre for Chinese vice, and, consequently, its capital of organized crime. Leading

gangsters shared with Shanghai industrialists a fear of what the Communists intended for their city and were anxious to reach some understanding with Chiang Kai-shek. They put together an army of hired muscle – the so-called China Mutual Progress Society – to attack the unions and militias of the left.

Above: Prisoners are roughly treated by Nationalist soldiers in Shandong.

In the early hours of 12 April, with the knowledge of Western representatives and the help of KMT units, this force launched a surprise attack on known left-wingers and union leaders, killing some and taking others prisoner. When, the next day, more than 100,000 workers came out on strike protesting these actions and demanding the release of those arrested, KMT troops opened fire with machine guns, killing 100 and wounding many more. In the ensuing 'Shanghai Massacre', 300 Communists were officially executed – although more than 5000 disappeared, their final fate never to be known.

China's eventual fate under Communism was not enviable, but even so, any sympathy for Chiang may be misplaced. If his fears of Soviet domination were justified, his way of dealing with the problem had been savage. The prolongation of his anti-Communist activities in Shanghai from this point on was utterly cynical, moreover: he and his henchmen denounced a number of wealthy merchants and industrialists as Red sympathizers, and appropriated their homes and property for their own use.

PUTTING DOWN THE PEASANTS

Over the next few years, Chiang's White Terror would extend beyond the ranks of the Communist Party to claim as many as 150,000 (perhaps a quarter of a million) lives. As a wry reminder of the socialist principles Sun Yat-sen had once espoused, homes, farms, tracts of land and business enterprises

SHADY SUPPORT

THE ROUTE FROM RELIGIOUS mysticism to criminal conspiracy may not be immediately apparent, but it was one that had been followed by several groups in Chinese history. Just as the Triads had ultimately been born out of the White Lotus sect, the Green Gang, the organization that controlled crime and vice in early 20th century Shanghai, was the descendant of an earlier Buddhist society, the Luojiao.

What had started out as a spiritual ministry among the boatmen of the Grand Canal took a more sinister turn when the Luojiao was suppressed under Qianlong. Its very existence now illegal, the society found itself in de facto alliance with Shanghai's salt and opium smugglers, and was increasingly involved in other illegal activities such as brothel-keeping and 'protection'.

By the 1920s, the Green Gang had taken charge of criminal life in this great seaport city. It saw the prospect of Communist rule – morally puritanical and economically restrictive – as an existential threat. On everything but the law and order issue, indeed, Green Gang leader Du Yuesheng ('Big Ears', 1888–1951) seems to have been sincerely conservative in his views. It had not just been opportunism that made him hire out his men to city businesses as strike-breakers; his support for Chiang Kai-shek over the Shanghai Massacre was evidently wholehearted. He would go on helping the Nationalist leader out financially for many years.

were 'nationalized' – shared out among the KMT leadership – with no compensation for their erstwhile owners.

Chiang's relationship with organized crime continued to be fruitful as the KMT's focus shifted to the countryside. Unrest was already endemic here, with the peasantry oppressed by landowners, for whom mafia-like gangs had long been acting as enforcers. Far from fighting for the people, the Kuomintang formed alliances with these gangs.

It was thugs of this sort who helped put down the Autumn Harvest Uprising, organized by the Communist leader Mao Zedong in Hunan province. For the Communists, it was a new departure in being a peasants' insurrection. Marxist orthodoxy did not accept that any real change could start with the peasantry – poor, uneducated and unsophisticated as they were and schooled over generations in superstition and social deference. Marx's revolution had to grow out of the radicalized anger of the industrial working class.

Mao's Autumn Harvest Uprising was an important departure, then. Although it may have been suppressed comparatively easily, it gave the Communists a new idea of how a revolution might be mounted. At the end of 1927, Mao's supporters retreated into remoter rural areas

and began establishing a presence among the poor at community level. First they won the people's trust, offering them practical assistance and advice, teaching literacy and generally making themselves indispensable to village life.

Mao Zedong himself had withdrawn into a mountainous region on the border between Hunan and Jiangxi provinces. With some 1600 supporters, he gained control over several villages, even setting up a Soviet ('council') of sorts. The experiment was never a complete success: several powerful families managed to hold out against his land reforms and attacks by KMT troops made life increasingly difficult.

Above: Mao (back row, third from left) poses with PLA comrades in Yan'an, in Shaanxi province, at the time of the Autumn Harvest Uprising.

Opposite: Thoughtful and contemplative, but something of a solitary ... As idealizations go, this picture of Mao could have been a great deal worse.

After a year, Mao gave up and moved his force deeper into Jiangxi, establishing his new headquarters in the town of Ruijin.

UNDER ATTACK

In Ruijin in November 1931, Mao set up the Jiangxi Soviet and was elected Chairman of the Supreme Council of a new Chinese Soviet Republic. This became a sanctuary for Communists suffering persecution elsewhere in south and central China. It also grew economically prosperous and militarily strong. As such, it represented a threat to those neighbouring districts under the tyrannical control of warlords, who lent their support to Chiang's increasingly rancorous anti-Communist campaign.

CHIANG KAI-SHEK'S ATTACK HAD NOT ONLY DEFEATED BUT DISPERSED THE COMMUNIST ARMIES.

The KMT leader attacked militarily in what should have been overwhelming strength, attempting to encircle and crush his enemy. Four times in succession, however, he was unable to land a real blow on a guerrilla force that seemed to melt away as he advanced. Finally, after emptying the area of people to ensure his supply lines and communications, he sent troops into enemy territory along newly built roads: this, his 'fifth encirclement', was successful.

A LONG RETREAT

Mao's Red Army had been so badly mauled that, as of October 1934, the Jiangxi Soviet could no longer be held. Chiang Kai-shek's attack had not only defeated but dispersed the Communist armies, leaving them isolated and vulnerable. Faced with total destruction, the First Front Army fled; three other armies were forced to leave their positions. In all, about 100,000 set out to make their slow and agonizing way to safety, circling east and northward under constant attack from the pursuing Kuomintang.

Cold, hungry, thirsty and sick, they suffered terrible privations: only a tenth of those who started were to make it, more than a year later, to the safety of Yan'an, in northerly Shaanxi province. Yet the 'Long March' was eventually mythologized as a heroic victory.

MODEST MAO

The father of rural revolution, Mao Zedong (1893–1976) was the son of a farmer, born and brought up in the countryside of Hunan province. His background had been comparatively comfortable, however; his father, although not rich, was by no means poor either. As his son, Mao had no experience, and little understanding, of the real hardships of those he was setting out to save.

Mao had no illusions about his ignorance. Patriotic pride had brought him to Nationalism; he'd embraced Marxism-Leninism at university in Beijing and made its adaptation to the Chinese situation his life's work. He appreciated how much he had to learn about the lives of the people and made a conscious effort to educate himself. What rules governed local markets? What role did religion play? How much land did the large estate owners own? For how much money did debt-ridden peasants sell their children? Armed with such detailed knowledge, he hoped to dispel potential tension over the land reforms he saw as necessary. He also worked hard at building up the Red Army, originally a disorganized collection of fighters who had come together in opposition to the National Revolutionary Army of the KMT. Mao quickly trained his troops up into a true guerrilla force. At this, the beginning of his career, the future Chairman showed no sign of the monstrous megalomaniac tendencies he was to manifest later as he grew in power. If anything, he was self-aware and humble.

MARCHING INTO MYTH

The Red Army does not fear the trials of the long March/
Taking ten thousand crags and torrents in its stride.../
The three Armies march on, each face glowing...

MAO, WHO WROTE THESE verses, knew just how outrageously they idealized what had actually been a horrendous ordeal. Only a handful of those who had started out had made it safely to Shaanxi after staggering the 12,000km (8000 miles) from Jiangxi. Most had fallen by the wayside as the armies slogged across a dozen mountain ranges or been swept away crossing the more than 20 major rivers on their route. Thousands, starving and sick, collapsed; more were killed in incessant skirmishes with the KMT troops who dogged their every step for months on end.

Years later, however, in his time of triumph, Mao revisited the experience and recast it as myth; the founding epic of the nation he was building. What the *Iliad* and *Odyssey* were to ancient Greece, what the *Aeneid* was to Rome, the Long March became to the Communists of China. Men such as Zhou Enlai (1898–1976), Lin Biao (1907–71) and Deng Xiaoping (1904–97) became Red China's equivalents of Achilles, Aeneas and Hector: they had been tried in the fire and finally emerged as heroes.

In the autumn of 1936, the last columns limped into Yan'an; within a year, the Communists would again be allied with the KMT. In July 1937, the Japanese mounted a full-scale invasion of China, moving south from their Manchurian colony of Manchukuo. While the Nationalists mounted a furious defence of Shanghai, it was taken after three months of ferocious fighting. Over a quarter of a million lives are believed to have been lost all told. Several thousand civilians were killed by accident when KMT planes mistakenly bombed the Shanghai International Settlement, inside which large numbers of refugees had taken sanctuary.

Shanghai having finally fallen, the Japanese moved on to Nanjing (then the Republic's capital), where they embarked on a six-week spree of rape and slaughter. Chiang Kai-shek's government was forced to fall back inland while the Japanese took Wuhan and Guangzhou – centres of industry and trade respectively.

For a time it appeared that China's Nationalists and Communists had put their differences aside in the face of this common foe. That was true up to a point, but the front was never as united as it seemed. Chiang Kai-shek could never bear

Opposite: Physically, of course, Mao's forces were drastically depleted. Mythically, though, the sculptor here was right: their march had made them heroes.

Below: Japanese troops make their way up a Chinese hillside during the Second Sino-Japanese War.

'THE RAPE OF NANKING'

THE SO-CALLED 'RAPE OF Nanking' (Nanjing) at the hands of the Japanese took place in 1937. It involved the violent deaths of more than 300,000 people over some six weeks, during which time between 20,000 and 80,000 girls and women suffered quite literal rape carried out by the invaders.

Soldiers prevented civilians from escaping while their comrades bayoneted or machine-gunned groups of people. The streets were left littered with decaying corpses. Archibald Trojan Steele of the *Chicago Daily News* saw 'a band of 300 Chinese being methodically executed before the wall near the waterfront, where already corpses were piled knee deep.'

'I witnessed three mass executions of prisoners within a few hours,' Frank Tillman Durdin of the *New York Times* reported. 'In one slaughter a tank gun was turned on a group of more than 100 soldiers.'

Japanese veterans later boasted of having taken part in killing contests, racing to see who could be the first to take a hundred lives.

Below: Japanese troops celebrate their victory at Nanjing. Today, recognition of the atrocity is a source of tension between Japan and its larger neighbour.

to abandon his fight against the Communists, however resolute his defence against the invader; nor could Mao's men resist extending their territories even as they fought a courageous guerrilla war.

By the beginning of 1939, the two sides were engaged in open conflict in many places, even as Japanese forces continued to stream into China from the north. They came together when it counted, however, that May massing at the cities of Suixian and Zaoyang, in Hubei province, where the Japanese had just arrived in considerable force. Counter-attacks by the Chinese saw the invaders first held and then forced to a standstill. Their initial advantage ebbing away as logistical problems and local guerrilla actions took their toll, the Japanese were losing confidence by the month.

This was before Japan's attack on Pearl Harbor, Hawaii, on 7 December 1941 had brought the United States and its Western Allies into what had by now become World War II. While the Russians attacked the Japanese in Manchuria, US and British forces fought an all-out war with them in the Pacific. (And, to some extent, in mainland China: more than 20,000 Chinese civilians are believed to have been killed in the US firebombing of Wuhan, in December 1944.) The Japanese remained in occupation in China, although increasingly beleaguered, until their general surrender after the atomic bombings of Hiroshima and Nagasaki in 1945.

MAO'S RED FORCES WERE VITALLY STRENGTHENED BY THE CAPTURED KIT THEY WERE GIVEN BY THE SOVIETS.

AN INCONCLUSIVE CONCLUSION

The final removal of the Japanese left the Communists and Nationalists scrambling to fill the resulting vacuum. The KMT had strong supporters in the United States. The Cold War was already under way and the Americans distrusted the motives of the Soviets – who came to the assistance of their Communist comrades. Mao's Red forces were vitally strengthened by the captured kit they were given by the Soviets – weapons and supplies the Russians had seized from the Japanese. But the Communists' key advantage seems to have been the 'hearts and minds' of the rural peasantry, won over by promises of ownership over their land.

By 1949, Mao and his Revolution had prevailed. The 'People's Republic of China' was proclaimed. Chiang Kai-shek and his chief supporters were forced to flee to the offshore island of Formosa (Taiwan). There, Mao's victory was pointedly ignored and a rump Republic of China remained in power, governed from a capital at Taipei. As far as the KMT leadership was concerned, their present difficulties were just a blip and

normal authority over the whole of China would soon be resumed. International opinion did not agree, however. Despite the backing of the United States, even Washington shared the general assumption that Chiang's Republic would soon fall. Instead, to the vexation of both sides, the PRC and the ROC have both endured; an uneasy accommodation has now been reached, it seems.

Left: Mao proclaims the People's Republic of China from the balcony of the Gate of Heavenly Peace, above Beijing's Tiananmen Square.

歡迎人民解放軍
大學

6

NOT A DINNER PARTY...

'Some classes triumph, others are eliminated. Such is history...' And such was the political philosophy of Chairman Mao.

Opposite: The entry of the Communist forces led by Mao Zedong into Beijing, 31 January 1949. Contemporary Chinese wall poster.

THE SLAUGHTER was not on the scale that Ren Bishi (1904–50) had called for – but then he had wanted 30 million deaths. That was the number of 'landowners and rich peasants' the Politburo's Secretary General said were squatting on the country, fattening themselves on the toil of China's poor. Mao himself had estimated that 'one tenth of the peasantry' would have to be 'destroyed' to allow the fresh start that was needed. Taken literally, that meant a figure in excess of 50 million. In the event, the death toll in Mao's campaign of innocuously titled 'Land Reform' (1947–51) fell some way short of either total. Western scholars are sceptical about numbers rising much above five million. Even so, the bloodshed was horrendous.

BORN IN BLOODSHED

This was a massacre the Party had specifically chosen to commit. 'Bliss was it in that dawn to be alive,' the English poet William Wordsworth (1770–1850) had famously written of a

Opposite: 'Political power grows out of the barrel of a gun,' Mao was notoriously to say.

French Revolution that had at least held its Reign of Terror in reserve for a few years. Mao, however, had decided that this was how he wanted his transformation of Chinese society to start: the slaughter was a declaration of intent. That he had so openly stated his aims suggests that he saw this kind of carnage specifically as a statement; a proclamation of how serious he was about bringing about real change.

If its victims were not 'innocent' in strict socialist terms, they were hardly all that guilty – only the tiniest proportion could seriously have been seen as 'rich'. For the most part, they had a little more than those around them – enough to make them feel like stakeholders, with property and a position to defend. In that regard, they may have been a brake on what the Party saw as progress. Even so, they cannot have wielded much power.

Below: A farmer kneels before a Land Reform tribunal, July 1952.

HORROR SHOW

It is hard to avoid the suspicion that Mao saw the murder of those people in the Land Reform as exemplary; as a warning to those inclined to obstruct his programme. To a certain extent, it was also an inducement to supporters – a recognition of the envy that many poorer peasants felt. 'Land reform' sounds like an enlightened end. As envisaged by Mao and his Party cadres, however, it was bloodily,

SINS OF THE FATHER?

IRONICALLY, THOSE TARGETED IN the Land Reform were families like Mao's own and those of his cadres – drawn disproportionately from the slightly more educated, more entitled-feeling ranks of the rural population.

Mao's father, Mao Yichang (1870–1920), had been born into actual poverty, in a village near Shaoshan, Hunan province. As a young man, however, he had been both industrious and canny, prospering as a moneylender and an entrepreneurial dealer in rice. His early hardships and subsequent success had left him with, on the one hand, an impressive work ethic; on the other, an austerely unforgiving attitude to the poor. Prudent to the point of miserliness, Mao Yichang was rigid in his views and strict in his discipline. All these things were to occasion quarrels in Mao's boyhood. While it is easy to see how such a father might have modelled a lack of moral imagination or empathy in his son, there is no real precedent there for the monstrosity of Mao.

Mao Yichang's inflexibility perhaps helps point the way to his son's excesses. The same could be said of Mao Yichang's lack of empathy. His son obviously shared this: despite his dedication to the cause of China's poor in abstract terms, he almost prided himself on his inability to relate to them as people. However, there was a world of difference between the small-mindedness of the self-made businessman Mao Yichang and the epic callousness to be shown by his mass-murdering son.

pointlessly punitive; a campaign of mass slaughter for mass slaughter's sake.

It was also committed for the sake of spectacle. In every village, once the 'class enemies' had been rounded up, they were paraded on a public stage before their communities. Abusively arraigned with their (often imaginary) crimes, they were beaten and then shot or sent to prison. Their homes were trashed, and their tools and livestock taken and distributed among their neighbours. The whole proceeding had a grimly festive feel.

ATROCITY AND ETIQUETTE

'A revolution is not a dinner party...' Mao had written in 1927. 'It cannot be so kind, courteous, restrained and magnanimous. A revolution is an insurrection, an act of violence by which one class overthrows another.' This was true enough, though the implication that a reluctance to exterminate people in their millions was on a par with fussing about conversation or table manners (Mao's were notoriously slobbish) is seriously contentious.

Again and again, over the coming quarter-century, Mao would resort to terror tactics much like these. Large-scale violence became a sort of shock treatment for the country; the

Below: Communist troops using captured Japanese weapons and equipment close in on Shanghai at the end of the Civil War in 1949.

A CRISIS IN KOREA

Above: General MacArthur senses victory at Inchon, September 1950, but the advantage gained here would be dissipated in the weeks that followed.

THE INVASION OF SOUTH KOREA by its northern neighbour, on 25 June 1950, upset the uneasy equilibrium that had prevailed in the peninsula since the expulsion of the Japanese five years before. From the Western point of view, the only thing to be said for southern strongman Syngman Rhee (1875–1965) was that, thuggish as he was, he wasn't the Communist dictator Kim Il Sung (1912–94), who ruled the North.

China's Communists don't seem to have been wild about their Korean comrade either. Nevertheless, they joined the war that autumn. As long as the South Koreans could claim that they and their Western allies were fighting defensively, Mao and his men preferred to steer clear of the conflict. But when the West went beyond this, they did become involved. There is no doubt that they were provoked. The bullish arrogance of General Douglas MacArthur (1880–1964) in invading the North was to upset his own president, Harry S. Truman (1884–1972). Even then, no Chinese territory had been violated, and Mao was in no way obliged to take his troops into the war.

Nor was Mao really equipped to, given the parlous state his country had been brought to by so many years of war – and by the destructive ravages of his own 'reforms'. But, just as it mattered to the Americans to support a Western-leaning ally, however unworthy of their help, it mattered to Mao to be seen as a champion of the anti-imperialist cause. China was intervening, not for Kim's sake, but for that of Mao's image as a liberationist inspiration for much of what was coming to be known as the 'Third World'.

In the event, the war ended in a stalemate, with the loss of almost half a million Chinese lives. But Mao had shown his steadfastness, so this represented a real result.

climate of fear it created would keep China on its toes. As many as 65 million people are believed to have been killed during Mao's reign – every one of their deaths an electrifying example for their neighbours and co-workers, their families and friends.

Even as the countryside was in the convulsions of this early Land Reform, the cities were being harrowed by the search for 'counter-revolution'. In 1951, for instance, thousands of former

TAKING TIBET

SINCE THE 16TH CENTURY, Tibet had been a semi-religious state presided over by the Dalai Lama, a Buddhist *bodhisattva*. That, at least, had been the theory: in practice, from 1720 on, the holy man had been a hostage, his country occupied by the forces of the Qing Chinese. Successive emperors had bundled the Himalayan state in with the other Central Asian regions on their western border as a source of trouble, to be dominated at all costs.

Below: The Chinese invade Tibet, as imagined by an Italian magazine of 1950.

So it seemed to Chairman Mao as well. After enjoying a period of autonomy from 1912, Tibet was invaded by the People's Liberation Army (PLA) in 1950. Such resistance as its scant forces were able to offer was quickly crushed, and Chinese sovereignty was asserted over Tibet. While a holdout group was to maintain a government-in-exile, based in India, where the Dalai Lama also fled, Tibet itself was taken under Chinese rule. There were benefits to begin with – the abolition of slavery and the most egregiously oppressive forms of serfdom, for example. Otherwise, Tibetan traditions were given some respect.

By the end of the 1950s, though, attempts at land reform in the spirit of the Great Leap Forward fostered resistance and rebellion in Tibet. As in China, the most obvious end result of Maoist

followers of Chiang Kai-shek who had handed themselves in on the back of a promised amnesty were condemned as counter-revolutionaries. 'Every day we would see the truckloads of prisoners,' one man – a student at the time – recalled.

While we were in our classes we would hear the terrible shooting. The trucks carrying away the corpses dripped streams of blood into the road that ran past the university buildings.

'modernization' was famine. Up to 15 million Tibetans are believed to have died. Attempts by Tibetans to fight for their freedom were put down by invading troops, whose repression was characterized by some Western observers as genocide. Their actions involved not only the massacres of civilians but the deliberate stamping out of Buddhist traditions. Monasteries were sacked and religious communities dispersed. Nomadic communities were wiped out. Harmless yak herders they may have been, but their peripatetic lifestyle seemed inimical to Communist ideas of order.

The repression was redoubled with the Cultural Revolution, to whose ethos Tibetan traditions seemed an outrageous affront.

Below: Insurgent monks surrender to the Chinese army, Lhasa, 1959.

'The history of all hitherto existing society is the history of class struggles,' Communism's founder, Karl Marx (1818–83) had famously declared. As far as Mao was concerned, however, history was in the here and now. As Party Chairman from 1949, he seems to have sought out conflict quite consciously and determinedly: 'Never forget class struggle,' was his slogan. The campaigns against landlords, rich peasants, the bourgeois counter-revolutionaries in the cities and all the other 'class enemies' went on and on. The Revolution had endlessly to renew itself, whatever self-destructive savagery that might mean.

The PRC's persecutions came to have a horrifically hyperactive feel. The price of success was ceaseless vigilance, its supporters claimed. A more cynical suggestion would be that the all-important thing was to 'look busy' for the boss. That the country paid the price for this in unremitting stress and trauma was not a problem as far as the revolutionaries were concerned.

Below: All smiles. Mao meets contented villagers on a visit to the countryside.

Chairman Mao seems to have been happy enough to see all these atrocities carried out in his name – for it was emphatically his name that loomed largest in Chinese life now. How far he saw his cult of personality as his narcissistic due and how far pragmatically, as the means to a political end, is not easy to decide.

Above: Schoolchildren study art – by copying the portrait of Chairman Mao that hangs on their classroom wall.

GAINING FACE

As the academic Daniel Leese has pointed out, Mao's self-presentation had been unassuming to begin with. In addition, there had been good reasons for Marxism-Leninism (an alien, Western concept) to be given a Chinese rebranding. Not only that: the memory of centuries of imperial rule could not simply be abolished at a stroke. Adulatory cults had grown up around earlier rebel leaders, such as Sun Yat-sen and Chiang Kai-shek. In his early years of power, officials had to go before Mao on his visits to villages to prevent the peasants from prostrating themselves before him. There is no suggestion that Mao craved this kind of adoration for himself.

But its identification with Mao in person gave Communism a Chinese face – quite literally, given that portraits of Mao were becoming ubiquitous. Images of the Party Chairman looked down from the wall in every government office, council chamber, classroom and public facility. Mao became the figure around whom a whole nation could be called to rally, and in whose defence any oppressive cruelty could be justified.

The cruelty too was something to be rallied around. Undoubtedly, it had its utility in sweeping aside resistance to the Party's aims, but it also had a hideous part to play as a bonding exercise. Whipped up to a collective frenzy, the Chinese people found themselves united in violence and loathing against a common (if only vaguely defined) 'class enemy'.

By the mid 1950s, it was no longer convincing that there could be an appreciable number of 'Nationalist saboteurs' or 'grasping landlords' left, so Mao decided to take another tack. The campaign he launched in 1956 to 'Let a Hundred Flowers Bloom' encouraged freedom of expression, both intellectual and artistic. The 'flowers' were supposed to be all the different imaginable schools of thought.

HUNDREDS OF FAMILIES WERE PULLED TOGETHER INTO LARGE-SCALE, COLLECTIVE ENTERPRISES.

However, when these 'flowers' did not all converge on the rightness of Maoist, Marxist socialism as Mao had expected, he took a violent swing the other way. The Anti-Rightist Campaign of 1957 took Chinese public life back to an already familiar formula: more purges, more angry propaganda, more show trials, as a (largely imaginary) movement of reactionary class enemies was rooted out.

FORWARD...AND BACK

While an already antiquated agrarian economy had been badly disrupted by the years of violent 'reform', no real progress had been made towards industrial development. In 1958, accordingly, China embarked upon the Great Leap Forward.

Although forced to cooperate with neighbours, sharing equipment and tools and helping each other out with labour, China's peasants had until now remained official proprietors of their own land. This changed with the Great Leap Forward, as hundreds of families were pulled together into large-scale collective enterprises, farming fields that were deemed the property of the state. This was a drastic and sudden transformation, and a lot to ask a particularly tradition-bound section of the population to adapt to.

There was resistance, although this was grist to the Communists' propaganda mill, creating as it did a new class of counter-revolutionaries. Their denunciation and punishment could be made a focus for public rage. Local activists organized 'struggle sessions', at which recalcitrant peasants were paraded before their communities to be yelled at and humiliated and beaten into confessing all sorts of antisocial activity. It was Land Reform all over again.

Above: Peasants toil together on a collective farm in this propaganda photograph.

MOBILIZED FOR MAO

In the meantime, armies of peasants were being set to work to help dig irrigation and drainage ditches and to extend the country's network of paved roads. Seeing a nation pulling together like this was, without doubt, a stirring sight. There was a downside, however: the more these people worked on infrastructure projects, the less labour they could expend on their regular agricultural tasks.

No matter; modernization was more important. Even more important than modernization was the perception that modernization was taking place. And even more important than that was the perception that it was doing so with the enthusiastic cooperation of the entire Chinese people under the heroic leadership of its Communist Party chiefs. Mao attached immense importance to the idea that every citizen should be involved in the construction of the future.

So, while vast steelworks were constructed to take the fullest advantage of the economies of scale and drag a backward economy into the 20th century, much smaller 'backyard furnaces' were also built. These sprang up in city neighbourhoods, on cooperative farms and in other odd corners; there were many thousands, the length and breadth of China. Local people brought their old bike frames, broken ploughshares, and even old pots and pans and other worn-out utensils to be melted down and processed into steel.

SHOW OF STRENGTH

The steel that the local manufactories produced was so poor in quality as to be unusable. The harder villagers worked on their furnaces, moreover, the less labour they could devote to their fields. Inevitably, agricultural output was hard hit.

Right: Millions were marshalled for ambitious infrastructure projects like this dam outside Beijing. But who was growing the rice they'd need to eat?

Mao didn't mind: what mattered most to him was the sense of a whole people toiling together with a common purpose, and the picture this painted of the Chinese Revolution for the outside world. There is no doubt that it was a magnificent sight to see so many millions of women and men committed to their country: foreign visitors marvelled at the scale and ambition of what was being done.

This was a revolution obsessed with its own self-presentation. If the Party media proclaimed record harvests, then record

Above: Mao and Deng Xiaoping, his right-hand man and (despite later disagreements) eventual successor.

harvests there had to be. If the rice wasn't there to justify such claims, the peasants had to be pilfering it. Many thousands of supposed 'thieves' were hauled out and shot; countless others imprisoned as saboteurs. That they were overwhelmingly innocent didn't matter: this too was theatre, of the cruellest kind. Likewise, officials who were not buoyant enough in proclaiming the triumphs of Mao's reforms were accused of disloyalty or 'deviationism'. They too were tried before kangaroo courts and executed or imprisoned.

Hundreds of thousands were to be killed this way. However, their numbers pale into insignificance beside the 46 million people believed to have died of starvation in the Great Famine that this Great Leap Forward brought about.

CALLED TO ACCOUNT

The People's Republic of China was not in any meaningful sense a democracy. The Communist Party did not have to fear any reckoning at the polls. Even so, by 1961, Mao's abject failures were catching up with him. Faced with mounting discontent in

LOVE OF LABOUR

Indefatigably driven himself, Mao had a major work ethic on his people's behalf. Despite his Marxist materialism, he seems to have seen labour as somehow sanctifying. Those dissidents who escaped execution were sent off in tens of thousands to special *laogai* camps (the name means 'reform through labour'). Other undesirables – thieves, drug-dealers, prostitutes, pimps and other 'parasites' – were sent for 're-education through labour' in a different set of camps.

There is much scepticism about the effectiveness of enterprises of this kind in rehabilitating inmates, whether ideologically in the *laogai* camps or socially in the rest. However, it was never really about the practicalities for Chairman Mao, but much more about the message he was sending.

the country, Mao's closest comrades were growing restive under his rule. These included men like Liu Shaoqi (1898–1969) and Deng Xiaoping (1904–97), Mao's friends since Civil War days, who had been with him at the time of the Long March. Liu was supposed to be Mao's right-hand man, his anointed successor as Chairman; Deng was another loyal supporter, but both were now signalling impatience with Mao's policies.

Their push towards a more moderate, slightly liberalizing economic and political approach was assisted by the fact that, in the Soviet Union, Stalin's successor Nikita Khrushchev (1894–1971) was heading in the same direction. Mao had openly condemned what he had seen as a softening of the Soviet Union's position in open Cold War conflict with the capitalist West. And, indeed, Deng and Liu's more conciliatory contacts with the Russian leader were not enough to heal this Sino–Soviet Split. Mao's paramountcy was clearly coming under question, however.

DESTRUCTIVE ZEAL

The 'Cultural Revolution' was aptly named, and what most would understand by 'culture' was in the firing line.

The Soviets had always taken seriously Marx's claim that the Communists were heirs to history: they had prided themselves in

Left: A Meeting of Russian and Chinese communist leaders in Moscow in 1960. Khrushchev is third from left, with Deng Xiaoping in the centre. Relations with the Soviets were comparatively warm by 1960.

VICTORY IN VIETNAM

The Chinese Communists had lent their support to their Vietnamese comrade Ho Chi Minh (1890–1969) since his country had formed part of the French colony of Indochine. In 1954, after battling with Ho's Viet Minh forces for more than a decade, the French gave up, despairing, and went home, leaving Ho Chi Minh the master of a Democratic Republic of Vietnam in the country's north. In the south, however, Ngo Dinh Diem (1901–63) held on in a separate Republic of Vietnam.

Notoriously now, the anti-Communist Americans rushed to Diem's support. They upped their commitment when the North Vietnamese intervened to help the Communist insurgents, the Viet Cong. The ensuing war has gone down in history as an American tragedy – even if US losses (some 60,000 lives) were dwarfed by those of the Vietnamese. America expected to prevail effortlessly, but was badly mauled. China's role has generally been underplayed, in part because such terrible events were taking place in China itself, in part because, within the region, support for another state in rebellion against 'imperialism' seemed self-evidently justified. But China was also consciously discreet about its contribution, its 300,000-odd troops in North Vietnam confining themselves to rear-echelon duties and freeing up the North Vietnamese Army for front-line roles. Their presence also inhibited the Americans, who bombed its Communist enemy heavily but were hesitant about intervening more directly on the ground. The victory of the North was a triumph for China, whose prestige in its Third World constituency was as much enhanced as the United States' was damaged.

their care in curating the cultural achievements of the past. They had turned the Winter Palace of the Czars into one of the world's most important art museums, the Hermitage; they had celebrated classic writing, and supported the ballet. Chinese Communism, as now formulated, was aggressively, self-righteously philistine, bent on creating a *tabula rasa* on which the glorious Red future could take form.

Opposite: Chinese militia members pledge their solidarity with Vietnam's struggle.

Art galleries, libraries, old cemeteries and shrines and historical monuments were vandalized, though in some cases concerned officials were able to save important sites. Antique books and manuscripts, paintings and prints were taken out into the streets and burned or otherwise defaced; statues and ceramics were smashed; innumerable unique artefacts were lost. Zhou Enlai was to walk a tightrope, publicly speaking up for the Cultural Revolution at Mao's side but working to curb the worst excesses of the Red Guards behind the scenes.

PURGING THE PAST

Mao's response was the all but automatic one for him of calling for a purge, claiming that class enemies were threatening the achievements of the People. But the Cultural Revolution was much more. It started off much as other crackdowns had, the Chairman summoning up all the old demons, denouncing

Below: Madame Mao brought an echo of the ancient past to modern China, recalling semi-mythic figures like Mo Xi or Daji.

Above: Young Red Guards honour their father figure, Chairman Mao (1966).

deviationism and revisionism; blaming bourgeois spies and saboteurs and the 'running dogs' of American imperialism for the People's woes. Thanks to the support of the so-called Gang of Four, however, Mao was able to make things happen – apocalyptically – on the ground.

Led by the Chairman's fourth wife, Jiang Qing (1914–91) or Madame Mao, this grouping also included hardline Mao supporters Zhang Chunqiao (1917–2005), Yao Wenyuan (1931–2005) and Wang Hongwen (1935–92). Themselves a generation or so younger than Mao and his old guard, they made this renewed revolution one of youth against established and hidebound ways. China, they insisted, was being held back by the 'Four Olds': Old Customs, Old Culture, Old Habits and Old Ideas. What was needed to set the revolution back on track was youth.

However, it was not the idealism of youth that they were most interested in unleashing but its unreflecting ignorance and headstrong recklessness. 'To rebel is justified', Mao had once said. The quotation was now dusted off for general – and just about universal – use. Called up in 1966, a new Red Guard made up of college and school students was given extraordinary powers to virtually take over China. Historian Jonathan Fenby cites a poster from this period with the elegant slogan 'Beat to pulp any and all persons who go against Mao Zedong thought.'

MAOIST MAYHEM

Beating people to pulp was just what the Red Guard did, on just about the slightest provocation. Attacking their teachers and ransacking their schools, they rampaged through towns and villages, having been given general licence to attack leaders of the old order and smash its institutions wherever they were found.

Classes were suspended so that a hundred million students could run amok. Even so many years after the first revolution, 'landlords' and 'rich' peasants were identified and liquidated; intellectuals (basically, anyone with any sort of education) were victimized. Officials were attacked, arraigned for cooked-up crimes of ideology at public struggle sessions and beaten or killed.

Mass rallies of Red Guards were held in Beijing and other cities. Over a million assembled in Tiananmen Square on 18 August 1966 to honour Mao. The Red Guards were given the run of the railway system so they could extend their influence far and wide. Gangs went off on violent joyrides around the country for months on end – so many that the nation's railway network was seriously overstretched. Goods piled up in transport depots, their distribution halted by the rise in rail traffic. More than 10 million tons had accumulated by the end of 1966.

Left: Red Guards in their tens of thousands mass for Mao in Tiananmen Square.

THE *LITTLE RED BOOK*

THE COLLECTION *Quotations from Chairman Mao Tse-tung* was first published in 1964, but it really took off at the time of the Cultural Revolution. A couple of hundred quotes to start with, it grew over time to contain 260-odd, representing the wisdom and insight of China's leader.

Mao never set up to be an Oscar Wilde, though he did at times attain a certain aphoristic dignity, as in his famous pronouncement: 'Political power grows out of the barrel of a gun.' He had imagination, too: his celebrated characterization of China's reactionary enemies as 'paper tigers' – nothing like as frightening as they first looked – has something of the character of poetry.

For the most part, though, his observations are unexceptional – leadenly earnest when they are not actually trite. 'Be resolute, fear no sacrifice and surmount every difficulty to win victory,' he says in one. What commander could conceivably disagree?

Such criticisms miss the point: the function of the *Little Red Book* was to be a talisman; a source of inspiration and an advertisement of allegiance. Billions of copies were eventually printed. At the time of the Cultural Revolution, key quotations were chanted aloud by enthusiastic crowds of students.

The effects spilled over into occupied Tibet and other frontier territories, whose people's adherence to local traditions – the very definition of 'Old' – was an affront to the new thinking. There were massacres in Mongolia and burnings of the Quran in Xinjiang. When a group of Muslim Hui, in Yunnan province, tried to break away from China in 1975, more than 1500 men, women and children were slaughtered by the PLA.

Mao's red star was back in the ascendant now. Under the guidance of Marshal Lin Biao (1907–71) – a military commander but also a talented practitioner of what we would now call public relations – his personality cult was bringing his status to almost godlike levels. The fortunes of Liu Shaoqi and Deng Xiaoping were consequently sinking. Of the rest of the Long March generation, Zhou Enlai (1898–1976) was the only politician to end the episode ahead. He had steered a careful course through the Cultural Revolution, staying on the right side of the Chairman and not giving the Gang of Four an excuse to denounce him while quietly steering the ship of state behind the scenes.

A GRIM LEGACY

Above: An avuncular-looking Mao smiles alongside his henchman Marshal Lin Biao in a propaganda poster from 1966.

Such chaos cannot reign for long without doing major and enduring economic damage, but this wasn't the only or most important impact the violence had. China emerged from the Cultural Revolution mentally exhausted and psychologically traumatized.

Given the geographical range the Red Guards covered, the anarchic nature of their spree and the extent of official collusion in their killings, it is impossible to give a reliable figure for casualties. Estimates vary wildly, from about 750,000 at the most cautious all the way up to 10 million – in truth, we just don't know.

There was to be a human cost beyond the killing and bereavement too: as the novelist Yu Hua (1960–) has noted, the former Red Guards became what amounted to a 'lost generation' in Chinese life. Not only were they lacking in education (they had effectively given up on school), they had been spoiled for the disciplines of the workplace too. In more sober, orderly times, they incurred the suspicion of the authorities, who distrusted the wild, freebooting spirit they seemed to represent.

GANGLAND

The Cultural Revolution had helped to make a star of Madame Mao, the former film actress Jiang Qing. She had revelled in the political limelight, soaking up the adulation of the Red Guards to whom she had orated at innumerable rallies, and her iconic appearance as 'Flagbearer of Proletarian Revolution' in propaganda posters. Her intimatc acccss to the Chairman placed her in pole political position even among the Gang of Four, who were starting to look like China's real rulers.

Lin Biao's death in 1971 cast a pall over Chinese politics. He was killed in a plane crash in Mongolia. Had he been defecting, many wondered? Party officials hinted as much, suggesting too that Lin had been involved in a coup conspiracy, though much about the incident remains obscure. Had he simply made himself so indispensable to Mao that he had, paradoxically, made himself a threat?

Whatever the truth, the episode seems to have diminished Mao. He stepped back a little politically now (though, well into his seventies, he could be forgiven for slowing down). Despite the continued mischief-making of the Gang of Four, the Cultural Revolution dropped down a gear or two. Zhou Enlai began to assert himself, backed by Deng Xiaoping (now back from the political wilderness) and the Marshal of the PLA, Ye Jianying (1897–1986).

Below: Madame Mao faces her accusers at her trial, 1976.

The grown-ups might soon be back in charge, it seemed. For that to happen, however, Mao would have to shuffle off the stage. In the event, Zhou Enlai went first, dying in January 1976. Nine months later, Chairman Mao himself died. While the Gang asserted themselves as his successors, within weeks, the moderates had moved against them and they were arrested and arraigned. Over 34 million deaths were laid at their door, which hardly seems unjustified, despite the inadequacies of what amounted to a show trial. They were to be shown more mercy, being given only lengthy prison terms (although Madam Mao was to kill herself in 1991).

BEIJING BARGAIN

MAO'S ABILITY TO MAINTAIN a position apparently above the political fray was perhaps best illustrated in his meeting with US President Richard Nixon (1913–94) in 1972. The violence of the Cultural Revolution was still continuing at this time. Nevertheless, the Chinese leader was thinking strategically.

Mao's reason for building bridges with the feared and distrusted American imperialists was to ensure security against the Soviet comrades he now feared and distrusted even more. Nixon's motives were much the same. Deeply distasteful as the Republican president may have found the idea of dealing with the PRC, he hoped to turn the Sino–Soviet Split to the United States' advantage.

In addition, a hawkish president with a grudging, even grumpy, air gained the credit for a bold and visionary diplomatic move. The visit was widely televised in America; Nixon's stock rose swiftly, as did China's. It helped that Nixon's hosts had dressed their sets for the occasion. Nice clothes, transistor radios and other consumer luxuries were issued to waiting crowds for the cameras' benefit (to be collected up again once the president and TV crews had departed), giving US viewers an entirely misleading glimpse of 'Chinese life'.

Right: 'The week that changed the world,' they called it. President Nixon meets with Chairman Mao.

CULTIVATING THE KILLING FIELDS

Above: The skulls of torture victims rest inside a stupa at the Killing Fields Museum outside of Phnom Penh.

NOMINALLY A MONARCHY, BUT in practice a colonial protectorate of France since the latter part of the 19th century, Cambodia was occupied by Japan during World War II. With the return of peace, Prince Norodom Sihanouk (1922–2012) proclaimed its independence. But France re-established its hold, and it was only after a bitter and lengthy liberation struggle, in which Khmer rebels fought alongside the Vietnamese Viet Minh, that Cambodia won its sovereignty in 1954.

The Americans saw Prince Sihanouk as being too sympathetic to North Vietnam and had him overthrown in a coup of 1970. This sparked off a five-year civil war, in which the Communist Khmer Rouge ('Red Cambodia') prevailed. Their leader, Pol Pot (1925–98), sought to build Communism on an agrarian, peasant base, like a Southeast Asian Mao Mark II. Another self-made magnate's son, his 'democratic' recipe for Cambodia was a cocktail of Maoist orthodoxy and an extreme, ethnocentric nationalism completely at odds with any of the teachings of Karl Marx.

As many as three million may have been killed during Pol Pot's reign of terror, whether through the murderous paranoia of the regime or its demented schemes of social engineering. In keeping with Khmer Rouge racial purity doctrines, minority

Above: Hanoi workers assert their readiness to resist the Chinese invaders, 1979.

peoples were wiped out, as were over-affluent and over-educated social groups. Entrepreneurs and professionals were slaughtered; entire populations were driven out of the 'decadent' cities to perform more fitting labour on the land. In many cases, their work here did not extend beyond digging their own mass graves. They were machine-gunned where they stood out in these 'Killing Fields'. As in Mao's China, the great economic experiment failed so spectacularly that enormous numbers of people simply starved.

China does not appear to have approved of Pol Pot's policies as such, but it had bigger geopolitical fish to fry. Despite Beijing's assistance through its war with the United States, Hanoi had been moving closer to the Soviets in the years since. When, in 1978, Vietnamese troops overthrew the Khmer Rouge, China responded by attacking across the North Vietnamese border, triggering a brief and inconclusive Sino–Vietnamese War (1979). The Chinese government claimed victory, although this seems to have been news to the Vietnamese, who remained in power within Cambodia until 1989. At this point, Prince Sihanouk returned as king. It was not until the Khmer Rouge were finally disbanded in 1999, however, that anything like normality was resumed.

HKEX
香港交易所

7

FROM MAO TO THE MARKET

The more things change in China, the more they stay the same, with the economic superpower continuing to be a place of poverty and repression.

A PROTÉGÉ of Zhou Enlai, Hua Guofeng (1921–2008) inherited the Party chair. Deng Xiaoping still had work to do to rehabilitate himself in ruling circles. Although Hua's quiet moderation was well received after the horrors of the Cultural Revolution, his loyalty to Mao made him too timid in his reforms. As the economy continued to languish, Deng Xiaoping's programme of more radical change grew ever more appealing.

The Maoist orthodoxy had been one in which every enterprise (indeed every possession – every tool, every teaspoon; in theory every grain of rice) had been publicly owned. Every aspect of economic life had been centrally directed from Beijing. Deng was now calling for a much freer and more open economy in which centralized direction would be drastically scaled down. Managements would operate with more autonomy; improvements in productivity would be rewarded with higher wages; energy and innovation would be incentivized.

Opposite: The Hong Kong Stock Exchange opens with an oriental flourish: capitalism and Communism have been hand-in-glove in the People's Republic too.

Above: Deng Xiaoping became a leading advocate for economic modernization after Mao.

Some private ventures were allowed from 1982. Prior to this, setting up a business had been – quite literally – a crime. The underlying morality had been clear. Trading for profit was intrinsically exploitative. By definition, it bought the worker's labour at a price below its real 'worth' (or it could not have been profitable); likewise, it charged customers above true cost.

Without this profit motive, though, why would anyone want to do business? Western capitalism saw self-interest as conducive to the general good. Entrepreneurs might ultimately be out for themselves, but to that end they offered benefits to everyone, through consumer choice, competitive pricing and innovation. Similar values would now prevail in the People's Republic of China, Deng proposed, albeit under state supervision.

If competition fosters creativity, it does so by rewarding enterprise, allowing those with drive and resourcefulness to 'win'. Inevitably, though, it leaves the rest as 'losers' in an inherently unequal system. In the West, under capitalism, these inequalities are usually accepted as it is argued that the whole of society benefits.

This was the view that China's modernizers took. It isn't hard, however, to see why an older generation of Mao loyalists saw it as a betrayal of everything they had fought for. They had struggled to build a society that provided for everyone, at least at the most basic level (the 'iron rice bowl'), not one that let a minority enrich itself at the poor's expense.

ENTERPRISE AND INEQUALITY

As if to underline the extent to which his changes were against the spirit of Maoist law, Deng now offended against its very letter. Communism was effectively suspended in the Special Economic Zones (SEZs) that he set up round the great old ports where foreign companies could operate freely. Not only would they be unhindered by the rigours of socialist central planning, but also they would not have to worry about the sort of regulation that would have restrained them in the West. This was all but unregulated, laissez-faire capitalism.

Below: Deng Xiaoping writes an inscription while visiting a business in a Special Economic Zone.

The irony was not lost on China's own older generation. They were offended not just ideologically but patriotically. The very conception of the SEZ was reminiscent of the kind of 'treaty port' the West had forced the emperors to open in the 19th century. Even so, successive governments were not to be diverted. On the contrary, since

Opposite: A poster proclaims the benefits of the 'one-child policy'.

the first of these SEZs were established in the early 1980s, dozens more have been set up in other ports – and, latterly, inland cities.

AN END TO ISOLATION?

Deng's modernizations did not just represent a departure from Maoist principles; they also reversed four centuries of Chinese isolationism. In a bid to introduce new skills and insights and to bring a backward country up to date, students were sent to colleges and universities around the world. Overwhelmingly, they went to study scientific and technical subjects rather than more ideologically unsettling ones in the humanities and arts. Nevertheless, they lived in Western cities, went to the movies, read magazines and books, and spoke with fellow students in campus cafeterias and coffee bars.

This loosening of the educational reins naturally encouraged hopes of greater intellectual and artistic freedom in China itself. It quickly became clear that the Party was not up for that, however, not least because it knew that demands for political liberty would inevitably follow.

Below: Emblematic as it was of the Chinese people's aspirations to democracy, the image of 'Tank Man' went round the world.

TIANANMEN TRAGEDY

The more freedom people were allowed, it seemed, the greater the clamour grew for still more, especially among the young. Campus unrest increased through the second half of the 1980s. The belief that Deng Xiaoping and the Party Chairman, Zhao Ziyang (1919–2005), were sympathetic to the movement only emboldened the liberalizers – and, of course, upset the conservatives further.

Public mourning for the death, on 15 April 1989, of another reformist statesman, Hu Yaobang (1915–89), turned

FAMILY AFFAIRS

MAO DID NOT FEAR nuclear war, he revealed in a notorious speech in 1957. China could lose half its 600 million population and scarcely notice. A source of strength in many ways, the country's enormous population was also a responsibility; even, in important ways, a liability. This was especially the case as China began to recover from the calamity of the Great Leap Forward: by 1970, the population was approaching 820 million.

Peasant parents have historically felt an imperative to have as many children as possible to help them work their plots and provide for them in their old age. High rates of infant mortality meant there was a sense of safety in numbers. In more developed societies, improving economic conditions and healthcare have largely removed this 'need to breed', leading to what has sometimes been referred to as 'industrial birth control'.

In China, however, this wasn't felt to be acting quickly or radically enough, so in 1979 a 'one-child policy' was introduced (it was lifted only in 2015). Parents were barred by law from having more than one child, and fines were levied on those who ignored the rule. The policy was widely condemned, for a variety of reasons. Some saw a violation of parental rights; others an attack on unborn, aborted foetuses, or even those putative children whose existence was pre-empted by contraception. Infanticide inevitably became a problem – one disproportionately directed towards baby girls. The state strongly disapproved of such sexism, but conservative, rural families felt that the importance of having a son outweighed the official line.

Beijing brazened out the criticism: the policy justified itself in myriad ways – from lower health and education costs to making food supplies go further. However, it may prove much tougher to deal with the longer-term problems China has created for itself through this policy. It has been apparent for some time that the country lacks the younger workers it really needs to keep the economy running, and to care for the vast numbers now in need of help in their old age. Then there are the consequences of favouring boy children: there is already a shortage of women, with implications not just for a generation of 'leftover' men (up to 50 million, it has been estimated) but for Chinese women who risk rape, abduction and imprisonment, and foreign women trafficked as 'brides'.

into a widespread protest movement in the weeks that followed. Thousands of people – mainly students and intellectuals but also ordinary men and women from every walk of life – started camping out in Beijing's central Tiananmen Square. They called for urgent political reforms, including the recognition of basic human rights and press freedom. An estimated 300,000 people had joined the protest at its height, around the end of May; there were similar protests in hundreds of other Chinese cities.

Then-premier Li Peng (1928–) responded by declaring martial law. In itself no great surprise (Li had always been a hardliner), this move came as a shock only because it was believed to have

Left: Locals inspect damaged vehicles in the aftermath of the Tiananmen trouble, 1989.

the backing of Deng Xiaoping. He was now apparently alarmed at what his policies had unleashed. Li Peng gave the order that the demonstrators must disperse, but something in the region of 100,000 still remained. The premier branded the pro-democracy campaigners 'counter-revolutionaries' and 'terrorists', despite the peaceful nature of their protest.

On 3 June, soldiers sent into the square with tanks opened up with automatic weapons. Over the following few days, while passive resistance to their advance continued, the PLA continued to clear the square and its surrounding streets, sometimes kicking and beating the demonstrators but also sometimes shooting.

Above: The son of a Long March veteran, Wang Jianlin represents a new kind of hero, with a net 'worth' of over US$20 billion.

By the time the crisis was over, several thousand protesters had been killed, along with a dozen or so PLA soldiers – mostly by accident or 'friendly fire'. The civilian death toll is unsurprisingly disputed: while Western claims that 10,000-plus were killed appear exaggerated, official suggestions that the figure lies in the low hundreds are not convincing.

GOOD TIMES...

These actions left the PRC a pariah, which was regrettable for the regime, although nothing new. Zhao Ziyang's replacement as Party Chairman, Jiang Zemin (1926–), did, as expected, maintain much tighter restrictions on political and cultural life, shrugging off continued criticism from the West. At the same time, he relaxed economic regulation further, doubling down on the policy of 'state capitalism' pursued before.

The ensuing 20 years saw China taking what might be characterized as a capitalist 'Great Leap Forward' to enter the 21st century an economic superpower. By May 2014, the country had more than 15 million private enterprises, their capital totalling over 100 trillion Yuan (almost US$17 trillion). The rate of growth was even more astonishing than its total scale: April 2014 alone had seen the establishment of more than 360,000 private firms.

By 2007, China had more billionaires than any other country, apart from the United States; by 2012, it had 212 billionaires and more than a million millionaires. This prosperity was 'trickling down' as well, as a new and growing urban middle class was enjoying a good life, full of high-end consumer goods.

BAD TIMES...

However, there were also reminders as to why so many in China had been drawn to revolutionary politics in the first place. Despite this new prosperity, these were not happy times for all. For a start, the boom was limited geographically, with a gap growing up between a coastal region readily accessible to foreign investment and an interior that was being left behind. By 2010, the per capita income in Shanghai stood at Saudi Arabian levels ($22,983); in inland Guizhou, in southwestern China, it was the same as India's, at $3385. Of China's ten wealthiest prefectural districts, eight were on the coast.

In public spending too, more was given to those who already had. Per capita expenditure on middle-school education in Beijing stood at 20,023 Yuan, for instance, as against Guizhou's figure of 3204 Yuan. Unsurprisingly, this imbalance was reflected in school leavers' illiteracy rates: 1.5 per cent for Beijing, but 12 per cent for Guizhou.

As for the rural population – still the overwhelming mass of China's people – the new prosperity was not reaching them at all. They were scratching a subsistence living, as they had been since ancient times. The mass of urban poor – a population that was rapidly growing, as young peasants streamed into the cities – also faced tough conditions. As *mingong* (migrant workers) there, they faced discrimination. The feudal *Hukou* system had still survived successive revolutions, and every peasant officially had to remain in the village community in which she or he had been born and registered. The migrants' ambiguous, extra-legal status made them ineligible for state support, so if they did not get the

Below: China's economic miracle has left numerous poor people behind, with shanty homes appearing on the edges of the great cities such as this one in Beijing.

DAMMED IF WE DO

POWERING THIS DEVELOPMENT DRIVE were more than 800 coal-fired power plants: these produced some 70 per cent of China's electricity – and enormous amounts of CO_2. China, while acknowledging these pollution problems, took exception to being told that it should be cutting back for the global good. After all, Britain, the United States and the other Western countries had not only enjoyed a century or so's headstart in industrial development, they had also been primarily responsible for the build-up in greenhouse gases.

Nineteenth-century history notwithstanding, it remained a reality that by 2014 China was responsible for 27 per cent of the world's carbon emissions. The need to rein these in was clear, as was the need for other energy sources to be explored (especially given China's poverty in oil reserves). The construction of the Three Gorges Dam, in the Yangtze Valley in western Hubei province, was one important venture of

Above: China's power plants have enveloped urban centres in a choking smog.

kind of high-paying employment for which they had moved (and, overwhelmingly, they didn't), they were forced to take whatever casual work they could. Thousands of sweatshops sprang up around China's cities, but if their owners were making money the *mingong* weren't. As the migrants' children were excluded from educational opportunities, the cycle of deprivation continued.

MARKET FORCE

The urban poor were vulnerable in other ways too, the slums and shanty towns in which they lived always liable to be bulldozed

this kind. Begun in 1994 and completed in 2012, the dam did not just generate energy: it played an important role in flood management and helped make the Yangtze River navigable over much more of its length.

However, the reservoir that formed behind the dam drowned vast areas of land – more than 1000 sq km (400 sq miles) – and displaced an estimated 1.3 million people. Their protests were put down, sometimes brutally. The rising waters also obliterated important archaeological sites, caused serious problems for local wildlife, and prevented the deposit of soil-enhancing silts further downstream.

without notice to make way for the construction projects, roadbuilding schemes and other large-scale developments that were a constant in this new and hyper-capitalistic China. A 'People's Republic' it may still have been, but it showed no more regard for the will or welfare of its citizens than it had in the days of Mao. Pleas for respect – or direct resistance – were given short shrift by the authorities, who favoured big business.

China never did foreground the individual in the way the West has done (in modern times, at least). Now, however, a contrast was becoming evident between this disregard for the rights of ordinary

Above: The Three Gorges dam produces over 100 billion kwh of electricity a year, but has brought with it major ecological, economic and social problems.

people and the range of consumer choices (if not political freedom) available to the middle class. Meanwhile, an already impoverished countryside was sinking deeper into desperation. The young and vigorous having left for the cities, only the old, sick and helpless were now left. The One Child Policy had already left an unfortunate imbalance between the generations. Young China's flight from the countryside could only make things worse.

GROSS PRODUCTS

China's economic growth has been spectacular, with its Gross Domestic Product (GDP) mounting steadily. Between 1978 and 2012, it was increasing at an average rate of 9.4 per cent a

Right: You can barely see the Shanghai skyline, so heavy is the haze of pollution that has settled on the city in recent years.

corner-cutting approach to industrial development and an unaccountable government prepared to look the other way. Regulation has been light to non-existent. The authorities have had their eye on the economic prize to the exclusion of just about every other consideration; grass-roots pressure groups, when they can even form, have been brusquely and often violently swept aside.

The consequences for the environment have been catastrophic. Pollution and environmental damage have affected not just the Yangtze dolphin (believed to have been extinct since 2002) or the numerous sites of special ecological interest or scenic appeal that

have been compromised, but the daily life of every Chinese citizen. China has more than 150 million cars and accounts for around half the whole world's coal consumption. Despite aggressive action in the last few years, barely breathable smog envelops all its major cities. This 'airpocalypse' contributes to more than a million premature deaths each year. Average life expectancy in the

Right: Even in rural areas, like this one in Guangxi Zhuang Autonomous Region, rivers and streams are heavily polluted.

DEMOCRACY AND DISOBEDIENCE

HONG KONG ISLAND HAD come to Britain as part of its plunder from the First Opium War. In the decades that followed, it had extended its colonial presence into 'New Territories' on the adjacent mainland. This arrangement had been formalized in 1898 when Britain took out a 99-year lease on the New Territories – the only thing that really made the colony viable thereafter.

When the lease ran out in 1997, Hong Kong could in theory have remained in British hands. For several decades, though, this hadn't seemed realistic. As early as 1984, London had bowed to the inevitable, agreeing to hand over the island along with the New Territories when their lease expired. In return, Beijing agreed that, for 50 years from that time, Hong Kong's British-style system – not just its capitalist economics but its democratic freedoms – would be respected. This was known as 'One Country, Two Systems'.

Over time, Beijing was to find it hard to stay detached, to the irritation (and fear) of democratic activists in Hong Kong. Interference in the political process and the harassment of opposition activists grew, until, in September 2014, students responded with a large-scale demonstration: 'Occupy Central with Love and Peace'.

Above: Hong Kong's last British Governor, Chris Patten, takes receipt of the Union Flag to mark the PRC's resumption of control over the colony.

A series of marches converged on Hong Kong's central district, where sit-ins were staged. Their violent suppression precipitated the Umbrella Revolution. This was so-called because protesters used umbrellas to defend themselves against the pepper spray the police deployed. By December, these protests had been put down, but while peace descended upon Hong Kong, nothing had been resolved.

Below: Students proclaim the so-called 'Umbrella Revolution'.

industrial north is a full five years lower than it is in the south of the country, largely because of air-quality issues of this kind.

RUNNING DRY

Water is at a premium, especially in the west of China: vast areas of what was once productive agricultural land have been left barren. More than 2.6 million sq km (1 million sq miles) is threatened by desertification of this kind, leaving the outlook grim for the 400 million people farming here.

Clean water has been still scarcer: two-thirds of China's 600-odd major cities experience shortages. Frequent chemical spills have polluted streams and rivers (more than a quarter of which have been deemed hazardous to human contact) – and, of course, the reservoirs from which people's drinking water comes. Less obvious, but just as damaging, is the chronic contamination of groundwater that, in 60 per cent of the country's urban centres, has been characterized as 'bad to

Below: Western singers like Madonna (here performing in Macau, China) have brought the Tibetan struggle into focus for a wide audience around the world.

very bad'. Unsafe drinking water is believed to have been a major contributor to cancers of the digestive system.

MORAL POLLUTION

Sometimes it has seemed that the regime is more concerned about cultural contamination and the decadence it discerns at the heart of Western life. Even the modernizers in Chinese ruling circles have tended to be comparatively old and culturally conservative. Where they differed from bourgeois fogies in the West was in their sense that a slippery slope led down from sexual and cultural freedoms to an existentially threatening open market in ideas and attitudes.

THE GOVERNMENT'S VIEW IS THAT TV SHOWS SHOULD UPLIFT AS WELL AS ENTERTAIN. THEY HAVE NO BUSINESS DEPICTING ANYTHING CONSIDERED 'DEVIANT'.

In January 2018, hip-hop culture and tattoos were banned from being shown on Chinese TV. The only surprise is that it took so long. After all, this was a media environment in which even extra-marital affairs were not supposed to be represented. The catalogue of prohibited, morally hazardous content, was very long. The government's view is that TV shows should uplift as well as entertain. They have no business depicting anything considered 'deviant', like drug-taking, prostitution or homosexuality; or even anything downbeat, like characters drinking to drown their sorrows or having casual sex.

It is easy to understand why singer Miley Cyrus posing for a photo with mock 'slanted eyes' in 2009 upset and angered people across eastern Asia. It is harder, perhaps, for Westerners to comprehend why the Chinese government then banned her music on this account. But China doesn't claim to be a liberal democracy; nor is its government embarrassed about making such rulings. That is in part what it is there for, it believes.

Other musical acts, from Oasis to Björk, have fallen foul of government sensitivities for making statements about the occupation of Tibet. And what the Chinese government really finds threatening about the international music scene, the media that reports it, and the internet that has become its portal is that it is potentially a portal for dissident ideas of every kind.

A TALE OF TWO TIBETS

SINCE THE START OF the century, Tibet has been among those Chinese provinces and autonomous regions benefiting from the China Western Development strategy. This has addressed some of the longstanding economic inequalities between coastal and inland regions, which have only deepened in the boom of recent years. But this has also been a way of strengthening Beijing's political hold over rebellious frontier regions – among them the Autonomous Region of Tibet. It is the colonialist convention to talk of the benefits brought by occupation. Once these would have been characterized as 'civilization'. 21st-century China has the self-awareness to speak instead of economic development. It can, however, point to the construction of the Qinghai–Tibet Railway, a continuing programme of roadbuilding, and the opening of new universities, hospitals and schools. Life expectancy has almost doubled under Chinese rule, from 35.5 in 1950 to 68.2 in 2017.

What, however, of the things that make life worth living, such as the Tibetans' language, culture, religion and traditions? China has rowed back from the contempt it showed during the Cultural Revolution era: the Tibetan language is tolerated, for

Below: Tibetan monks take part in a prayer festival in Kathmandu, Nepal.

example; it is even spoken on official TV channels. Attempts have been made to preserve and restore the country's religious heritage, to look after Buddhist monasteries and shrines.

Where Tibet's unique historical heritage starts shading over into actual, present-day differences of identity and aspiration, however, Beijing's attitude becomes more grudging. And where these aspirations give way to anything resembling political activism, the reaction has been hostile and heavy-handed. In 2008, a wave of protests was put down with what international agencies believe was excessive violence; many people were imprisoned for peaceful activism. In the years since, protests have continued. Scores of monks and nuns (and lay protesters) have committed suicide by setting fire to themselves, in Tibet itself and in Chinese city squares.

Demonstrations and religious ceremonies have been disrupted; known activists prevented from travelling or arbitrarily detained. As of 2018, there were believed to be 300 Tibetan political prisoners. There were widespread reports of torture; some activists simply disappeared.

Below: Tibetan protestors march for freedom, their English slogans a reminder of the international traction their struggle has gained.

WORLD WIDE WORRY

Since the arrival of the internet in the early 1990s, China's attitude has been ambivalent. On the one hand, it naturally wished to make the most of a transformative commercial tool and a vital avenue of scientific and technological development. With its help, Chinese institutions and enterprises could access cutting-edge academic research into everything from metallurgy to medicine, and up-to-the-minute data on everything from commodity prices to local tariffs and regulations. On the other, discomfort was felt with the internet's corollary function as a forum for the free flow of media, imagery and ideas.

Its greatest admirers admit that a lot of pernicious material circulates on the internet, from fraudulent financial schemes to child pornography. What isn't actively harmful is often still unedifying. What was conceived as a high-minded medium by which academics could compare notes on research and communicate their findings across a global community has apparently found its true level with pseudoscientific health fads, celebrity gossip, prank videos and kitten memes – and, in a more sinister vein, conspiracy theories and fake news.

While China at first struggled to find a response and ended up being liberal by default, allowing internet users more or less

Below: China's younger citizens have been enthusiastic adopters of the internet, like those we see in this internet café in Chengdu, 2011.

INFO WARS

STORIES OF TEENAGE HACKERS operating out of suburban bedrooms finding their way into the Pentagon's computer systems were a source of entertainment for the naive 1990s. But it wasn't long before the mood began to darken as people realized that what was possible for mischievous geeks might be possible for hostile regimes as well.

Above: US Deputy Attorney-General Rod Rosenstein briefs the US press on attacks by Chinese hackers on scores of companies in a dozen countries.

While the US was the primary target, the governments of countries from Canada to Norway and from Australia to India have complained of hackers interfering with their systems. Organizations like Yahoo and Google insisted that their systems had been violated by Chinese hackers and used to facilitate cyber-surveillance or information theft. Designated units of the PLA were tasked with penetrating Western cyber-security, stealing secrets and planting compromising malware.

Aerospace corporations like Boeing, Lockheed and Northrop were cyber-raided for details of both military and civic projects. In 2010, China Telecom's diversion of US internet traffic on to its own networks for a matter of minutes was enough to give it access to enormous volumes of important data.

Soon, however, it became clear that this kind of cyber-spying was just the start; there was all but limitless scope for cyber-sabotage as well. The sort of 'smart' systems in use these days for handling everything from water and electricity supplies to air traffic control and railway signalling were sitting targets for an online enemy.

free rein, it has tightened things up considerably since the turn of the century.

The Golden Shield Project (known more colloquially as 'The Great Firewall of China') now allows 'unacceptable' content to be excluded. It equips an army of 50,000 censors to restrict the scope of search engines so forbidden materials don't come up, or bars access to specific websites. The censors can also monitor the online activities of every citizen, seeing exactly what they are searching or what they are saying to their friends online. In the meantime, the kind of 'influencers' who in the West are modelling fashion and lifestyle choices make themselves poster children for loyal citizenship.

AN EXPLOITATIVE EMPIRE?

China's revolutions, Nationalist and Communist alike, have defined themselves against Western imperialism. Mao saw himself as a champion, not only of his country's dispossessed, but of a Third World ravaged by centuries of European and US colonial oppression. That this solidarity continues is shown, the PRC contends, by its investment in developing countries – especially those of Africa.

Below: China rolls out the red carpet for President Idriss Deby of Chad, in Beijing for the FOCAC summit, 2018.

Established in 2000, the Forum on China–Africa Co-operation (FOCAC) has none of the ostentatious pomp of the 15th-century Treasure Fleet, but is just as overbearing, Western critics have complained. More than 800 companies have been involved – private firms but, in the true spirit of state capitalism, strongly backed, financially and politically, by

Above: The Colombo Port City project in Sri Lanka has been built with Chinese money. This is part of an estimated $5 billion lent by Chinese banks to Sri Lanka, which has helped build a new port, a new airport and a railway on the south coast.

the government. Along with prestigious public buildings, they have funded and managed important infrastructure projects, constructing roads, railways, airports and hydroelectric schemes. They have invested in bauxite exploration in Ghana, oil refineries in Nigeria, lumber enterprises in the Congo and Cameroon, Manganese mines in Gabon and South Africa, chromium extraction in Madagascar and Sudan, and copper, gold and iron mining in Zambia, Tanzania and Mozambique.

China clearly stands to benefit from these projects in the longer term – but the same would be true of Western enterprises investing in the region. Typically, the Chinese point out, they have provided more advantageous credit terms than Western companies, and low-interest loans that European and US banks would never have entertained. The question is, what does China hope to gain from what some see as low-key colonialism? And, conversely, what – apart from important investment – are African countries going to gain from this relationship? It won't be liberal democracy – but then Western investors generally haven't brought this either. However genuine the freedoms enjoyed by their own peoples back in Europe or North America, they have often been content to see African countries under the control of kleptomaniacs and monsters.

COLONIALISM AT HOME

China's hold on Xinjiang in its far west, slowly strengthening since the 18th century, seemed pretty firm by the turn of the millennium. The Dzungar had long been annihilated, while the surviving Uighur population was now outnumbered, thanks to the continuing state-sponsored settlement of Han Chinese and the exodus of some 60,000 Uighurs, uncomfortable or

Below: Muslims in Jakarta, Indonesia, protest their Uighur co-religionists' persecution in the PRC, where more than a million may have been interned.

fearful under Chinese rule, to the comparative safety of central Asian republics such as Kazakhstan, Uzbekistan and Kyrgyzstan.

The Uighurs were set apart both by their Turkic ethnic, cultural and linguistic background and by the Islamic faith they had followed since around the 16th century. Although most were not nomadic, many felt sufficiently alienated from Chinese ways to want their independence in a separate state of Uyghurstan. China's response was always going to be robust. Mosques were destroyed, meetings broken up and activists harassed over many years. Since 2014, however, the authorities have been rounding up Uighurs (and members of other Muslim groups) without trial or even charges and herding them into 're-education' camps.

SHE WAS BEATEN TILL SHE BLED AND SUBJECTED TO ELECTRIC SHOCKS.

Information about what China has been up to in secrecy in one of its remotest regions has been in short supply. Even so, the international press has followed the developing situation as closely as it can. China has denied these camps' existence (or, in some cases, explained them away as 'vocational training centres'), but United Nations estimates suggest that a million or more people have been interned.

AN OPEN-AIR PRISON

The entire region has been characterized as an open-air prison, and Tarim Basin's biggest city, Hotan, 'feels as if it is under siege', says the *New York Times*'s Chris Buckley. China denies any racial animus against the Uighurs, so resents the suggestion that it has created a complex of Nazi-esque 'concentration camps' – indeed, it is overwhelmingly on account of political deviation or disloyalty that men and women become targets.

This in its turn brings the imperative to 're-educate' – to ensure that inmates undergo a change of attitude. The only effective way of getting men and women to renounce (or say they do) their deepest emotional allegiances is to force them to through torture. Reports of this abound. One former inmate, Mihrigul Tursun, testified to the US Congress in November 2018, describing how she was beaten till she bled and subjected to electric shocks that threw her whole body into convulsions.

Official tactics, Buckley says, are 'reminiscent of those of Mao's draconian rule – mass rallies, public confessions and "work teams" assigned to ferret out dissent.' But Mao's people never had the benefit of modern metal detectors and biometric data collection to assist them in their repressive work. Facial-recognition systems developed here to keep track of inmates who, having been 're-educated', have been released, have been sold to other states such as Zimbabwe. Not that the PRC have been the only ones to make a profit out of mass repression: Western companies like Microsoft have also been accused of assisting in these schemes.

'EVERY TOOL THAT A FUTURE, LARGER TOTALITARIAN STATE MAY USE TO CONTROL CITIZENS IS CURRENTLY BEING TESTED IN XINJIANG.'

The prospects looking forward are still more disturbing. The situation was summed up by the *Washington Post*'s Anne Applebaum: 'Every tool that a future, larger totalitarian state may use to control citizens is currently being tested in Xinjiang.'

DARK DAYS?

Far from promoting social cohesion, the prosperity of China in the past few decades has only heightened the need for repressive policing to maintain order. Sophisticated social management, underwritten by brute coercion, is needed for Chinese society to go on functioning.

Even allowing for the stereotyping to which the Chinese have been subjected for centuries, theirs has never really been a free society. Western democracy may have been flawed in many ways, its accountability to ordinary people much exaggerated, and its fullest liberties available only to the few, but China's extraordinary civilization has grown and flourished without encouraging the sort of individualism to which the West has aspired in recent centuries. At its best, its history has always had a dark dimension, and there is no reason to think that this is at an end.

Opposite: Police stand guard in a shopping centre in Hotan, Xinjiang, where tensions continue between the minority Uighurs and the authorities.

BIBLIOGRAPHY

Becker, Jasper. *Hungry Ghosts: China's Secret Famine* (London: John Murray, 1996).

——. *The Chinese* (London: John Murray, 2000).

Ebrey, Patricia Buckley. *The Cambridge Illustrated History of China* (Cambridge: Cambridge University Press, 1996).

—— (ed.). *Chinese Civilization: A Sourcebook* (New York: Simon & Schuster, 2009).

Fenby, Jonathan. *The Penguin History of Modern China: The Fall and Rise of a Great Power, 1850–2008* (London: Allen Lane, 2008).

Heidhues, Mary Somers. '1740 and the Chinese Massacre in Batavia: Some German Eyewitness Accounts', *Archipelago 77*, 2009, pp. 117–47.

Hung Ho-fung. *Protest with Chinese Characteristics: Demonstrations, Riots, and Petitions in the Mid-Qing Dynasty* (New York: Columbia University Press, 2011).

Kroncke, Jedidiah Joseph. *The Futility of Law and Development: China and the Dangers of Exporting American Law* (New York: Oxford University Press, 2016).

Kuhn, Philip A. *Soulstealers: The Chinese Sorcery Scare of 1768* (Cambridge, Mass: Harvard 1990).

Lee Khoon Choy. *Pioneers of Modern China: Understanding the Inscrutable Chinese* (Singapore: World Scientific Publishing, 2005).

Leese, Daniel. *Mao Cult: Rhetoric and Ritual in China's Cultural Revolution* (Cambridge: Cambridge University Press, 2011).

Makeham, John (ed.). *China: The World's Oldest Living Civilization Revealed* (London: Thames & Hudson, 2008).

Perdue, Peter. *China Marches West: The Qing Conquest of Central Asia* (Cambridge, Mass: Harvard, 2005).

Portal, Jane and Duan Qingbo. *The First Emperor: China's Terracotta Army* (London: British Museum Press, 2006).

Rummel, R.J. *China's Bloody Century: Genocide and Mass Murder Since 1900* (Piscataway, NJ: Transaction Publishers, 1991).

Scarre, Christopher. *The Human Past: World Prehistory and the Development of Human Societies* (London: Thames & Hudson, 2009).

—— and Fagan, Brian M. *Ancient Civilizations* (London: Routledge, 2008).

Simmons, Diane. *The Narcissism of Empire: Loss, Rage and Revenge in Thomas de Quincey, Robert Louis Stevenson, Arthur Conan Doyle, Rudyard Kipling and Isak Dinesen* (Eastbourne: Sussex Academic Press, 2007).

Stringer, Chris and Andrews, Peter. *The Complete World of Human Evolution* (London: Thames & Hudson, 2005).

Wasserstrom, Jeffrey N. (ed.). *The Oxford Illustrated History of Modern China* (Oxford: 2016).

Wood, Frances. *Did Marco Polo Go to China?* (London: Routledge, 1996).

——. *No Dogs and Not Many Chinese: Treaty Port Life in China, 1843–1943* (London: John Murray, 2000).

——. *The Silk Road: Two Thousand Years in the Heart of Asia* (Berkeley: University of California Press, 2002).

——. *The First Emperor of China* (London: Profile, 2007).

Yu Hua. *China in Ten Words* (New York: Pantheon, 2011).

Zimmermann, Jean Turner. *Chicago's Black Traffic in White Girls* (Chicago: Chicago Rescue Mission and Woman's Shelter, 1911).

——. *The Social Menace of the Orient*, Volume II (Chicago: Chicago Rescue Mission and Woman's Shelter, 1921).

INDEX

Page references in **bold** refer to illustration captions.

PICTURE CREDITS

Alamy: 5 (Keith Levit), 8 (Chronicle), 10 top & bottom (Archive PL), 15 (Heritage Image Partnership), 16 (The Picture Art Collection), 18 (Chronicle), 21 (Science History Images), 23 (Photo 12), 24 (Lebrecht), 26 (National Geographic), 27 (Universal Art Archive), 30 (Picture Art Collection), 33 (Chronicle), 34 (Artokoloro Quint Lox), 36 (charistoone-images), 37 (Zuma Press), 42 (Danita Delimont Creative/Kymri Wilt), 46 (Science History Images), 51 (Keith Levit), 54 (The Picture Art Collection), 57 (Classic Image), 58 (Lou-foto), 72 (Michelle Gilders), 73 (Classic Image), 74 (Artokoloro Quint Lox), 76 (Heritage Image Partnership), 77 (Artokolor Quint Lox), 78 (Interfoto), 80/81 (Chronicle), 89 (Classic Image), 92 (Interfoto), 93 (Classic Image), 94 (Chronicle), 95 (GL Archive), 99 (History & Art Collection), 100 (FLHC Maps 9), 103 (Raymond Asia Photography), 108 (Painters), 110 (Culture Club), 112 (The Picture Art Collection), 113 (Art Collection), 115 (The Picture Art Collection), 117 (Classic Image), 126 (Historic Collection), 127 (Classic Image), 130 (Chronicle), 133 (The History Collection), 134 (Heritage Image Partnership), 136 top (Chronicle), 136 bottom (Archivart), 141 (Vintage Archive), 144 (Ian Cruickshank), 151 (Everett Collection), 164/165 (Photo 12), 168 (Everett Collection), 172 (Chronicle), 177 (Photo 12), 186 (Prisma by Dukas Presseagentur), 187 (Peter Probst), 189 (Everett Collection Historical), 194 (Keystone Press), 197 (Barry Lewis), 200 (Lou Linwei), 201 (Panther Media), 202 (Tao Images), 206 (Newcom/B J Warnick), 207 bottom (Jayne Russell), 214 (Xinhau)

Alamy/Granger Historical Picture Archive: 11, 13, 41, 53, 67, 105, 139, 140, 145, 153, 159, 166

Alamy/World History Archive: 6, 32, 40, 75, 91, 119, 142, 162, 181

Amber Books/Art-Tech: 35, 63, 64, 79, 86, 87, 88, 96, 101

Bridgeman Images: 9 (Look & Learn), 47 (Look & Learn/Angus McBride), 49 (DeAgostini), 52 (Pictures from History), 60, 68 (Biblioteque Nationale), 70, 97 (Pictures from History), 120 (Victoria & Albert Museum), 125, 128 (DeAgostini/Maritime Museum, London), 137 (UIG/University History Archive), 157 (Sovfoto/UIG)

Dreamstime: 38 (Jess Yu), 48 (Nick86174), 160 (Song Yang), 190 (Stefano Ember), 210 (Dimaberkut), 212 (Piero Cruciatti)

Getty Images: 14 (DeAgostini/Biblioteca Ambrosiana), 28 (National Geographic/O.Louis Mazzatenta), 104 (China Photos), 122 (Print Collector), 132 (DeAgostini/M. Seemuller), 146 (DeAgostini Picture Library), 149 (Hulton Archive), 154 & 155 (Hulton Deutsch), 161 (Ullstein Bild), 169 (Bettmann), 170 (Keystone), 173 (Bettmann), 174 (Keystone–France), 175 (Mondadori Portfolio), 178/179 (Keystone-France), 180 & 182 (Bettmann), 183 (Sovfoto), 184 (JEAN VINCENT), 185 (Agence France Presse), 188 & 191 (Sovfoto), 192 (AFP/Anthony Wallace), 195 (AFP/Xinhua), 198/199 (Peter Charlesworth), 207 top (Emmanuel Dunand), 208 (Visual China Group), 211 (AFP/Prakash Mathema), 213 (AFP/Nicholas Kamm), 215 (Paula Bronstein), 216 (NurPhoto), 219 (AFP/Greg Baker)

Library of Congress: 143

Photo Dharma: 29 (Creative Commons 2.0 Generic)

Rex by Shutterstock: 196 (AP/Jeff Widener)

Shutterstock: 17 (Fotokon), 31 (Vlad Sokolovsky), 50 (DuDavis), 84 (Peter Zachar), 203 (Jejim), 204/205 (Hung Chung Chih)

US National Archive: 171